Resurrecting TV News

A Digital Plan for the Broadcast Afterlife

Nick Winkler

THE WINKLER GROUP
STRATEGIC COMMUNICATIONS

www.thewinklergroup.net

Also by Nick Winkler

Break Out of PR Prison: Make & Measure Your Own News in an Era of Crisis

To Frank Currier,

Well done, Sir.

Thank you.

I'm sorry.

-NRW

Contents

Contents

Nick Winkler

Dear TV News,

I love you…
But like many before me- I'm breaking up with you.
Don't get me wrong…
What we had was great and will always be special to me.
But it's just not enough anymore.
I need more from a relationship than you're willing to give.
What I'm trying to say is…
It's not you- it's me.
You're pretty much the same as when we first met.
I'm the one who has changed.
I didn't want it to happen…
But I've fallen in love with someone else.
He's always there for me.
And he lets me be me.
I know, I know…
It sounds weird but he gives me the freedom I've always dreamed of.
Whenever I feel like seeing him, I call him up.
I spend as much or as little time with him as I want.
He doesn't force me to see him at a certain time.
He doesn't require me to listen to what he thinks is important.
No, he allows me to choose where and when we see each other.
And what we do.
That's something I've gotten use to.
And I'm just not sure I can go back to the way it was with you.
I'm not trying to be mean…
It's okay, you keep doing your thing.
But you're a little bossy and a little boring for me.
Especially when you tease me before going away for a break.
It's just not cool, you know?

Or when you try to scare me into paying attention to you…
That's just not nice.
And on the rare occasions I do spend time with you…
I sort of feel like what's the point, you know?
You're pretty predictable.
My new love is nothing like you.
In fact, he's confident enough in himself to let me be me.
To show me things he didn't create but thought I might like.
He trusts me to wander around by myself knowing I'll come back.
He respects me and my time.
I mean, it really bothered me when you insisted we see each other at 5 and then again at 6 each night…
At least change it up a little at 6, you know?
And why do you only dress up and pay attention to me 4 months out of the year?
I deserve your best every day of the year- not just when you think it counts.
I'm sorry if this hurts.
I just figured I'd be honest.
Maybe then you'll take an honest look at what you've become.
Or what you haven't become.
Maybe it'll help you grow.
Don't get me wrong…
My parents REALLY loved you…
And they're not sure about the new love I've found…
But I have to do what makes me happy.
It is about me, you know?
Okay, I know it has been a rough time for you and your friends lately.
Rejection and change are tough.
But you guys can't keep acting the way you always have.
I don't mean to lecture you.

Nick Winkler

I just want the best for something I used to love and will always hold dear.

So think about what I've said.

But don't call me—I prefer to text.

Maybe one day we can be friends again.

But right now it's kind of awkward...

So I'll probably just ignore you.

K?

It's okay to cry- no one's watching.

b-good

cu L8tr

Love always,

-The Ex-Viewer

Disrupting the Disruptors

Stop trying to boost your newscast ratings. It's not working, it hasn't worked, and it won't work. At least not materially or the way you're executing.

Even if you're a news director in a swing state and enjoy a political advertising boom every two years and an even larger cash cow every four, the slow but consistent decline in local television news ratings is a threat growing in tenacity.

The solution most in the industry try...

Insanity!

Television news continues to try the same things, with minor tweaks, and expects different results:

- Sweeps pieces that attempt to scare viewers into watching
- Break out elements comprised of nothing more than an archive or Google search
- Requiring reporters to show more personality and movement to compensate for pointless live shots or a lack of content

How'd that work out for network affiliates in 2012? *The Pew Research Center's Project for Excellence in Journalism* released its *State of the News Media 2013* report and compiled this list of highlights:

- Viewership fell, on average, 6%
- 1 in 3 people has stopped watching a particular news outlet
- Higher-earning individuals as well as younger viewers are turning away at even higher rates

Have a heavy bottle handy if you choose to read the entire report here: http://stateofthemedia.org/

I know what you're likely thinking…

But until you learn to smartly monetize your website, smartphone application, and tablet adaptation, increased website traffic is meaningless.

If you doubt this please revisit the dot-com bubble where eyeballs were mistaken for outcomes.

The metrics you choose to measure yourself with will determine, in part, whether you earn a place at the media table of the future.

Before I continue let's be clear about one thing. This book is not for people who believe the following:

- Those who believe incremental change will do
- Those who believe they've already gone digital
- Those who still create sweeps pieces 4 times a year
- Those who still use the term sweeps
- Those who believe they've already created the "newscast of the future"
- Those who consistently rely on focus groups
- Those who rely solely on gut, intuition, and emotion

If one of the aforementioned bullet points describes you, chances are you will fight, resist, and denounce the pages that follow.

If so, please stop reading and get back to the all-important task of tinkering with your newscast.

But if you're willing to completely reimagine television news, the rest of the book was written for you. However, before proceeding you must agree to the following:

- I will treat this manifesto not as a map but rather a compass
- I will tweak, alter, and add to it
- I will misuse it
- I will subtract from it
- I will embrace the discomfort it prompts
- When I fail I will fail smart and quickly
- I will rely on it only when I cannot do it a better way
- I will use it as a part of the creative process but not as a replacement for it
- I will treat it as a prelude to reinvention rather than a substitute for it

The car we've been riding in has broken down.

There has been a major failure.

While many continue to crack the hood and make minor repairs that allow the car to continue limping along, those who are honest with themselves understand a major overhaul is in order.

Repairs will not suffice.

Instead, we must find the courage to tear off the hood, pull out the engine, and install a brand new one.

One that has not yet been invented.

One that does not come with a manual, map, or how-to guide.

Nope, we're creating from scratch.

Technical know-how is secondary in this task. More important is finding the courage and overcoming the fear that'll come with creating something brand new, unique, and isolated from its peers.

The best selling business books of our time often outline strategies designed to disrupt a given industry. The first to successfully disrupt generally prospers. However, our industry has already been disrupted.

It's our job to disrupt the disruptors.

The Lonely Future

You'll notice the book is written for those producing television news.

More specifically, this book is for those who wish to produce a next generation news product.

However, this book completely ignores a television station's role as a network affiliate. The purpose of this book is not to convince you that television networks, as we know them, will no longer exist in the near future.

That debate will not be settled here.

Even those owning and operating network affiliates will acknowledge the industry is undergoing rapid change in terms of content distribution. If you do not believe that granting anyone with a connection to the web the authority to distribute content is, at the very least, a potential threat to the longevity of network affiliates, I urge you to stop reading right now.

Again my goal is not to lecture or convince.

It is to prepare.

If the prospect of no more affiliates is even a remote possibility you've considered, then it is your responsibility to prepare for an affiliate-free future. The idea that one day you might be left with only your local newscast is one worth considering even if you do not believe the current network affiliate structure is being threatened.

Why?

Preparing for a future where your only bread and butter, at least for a time, is your newscast will only serve to make your news product better. It's a win-win situation. Whether you believe in the survival or demise of the network affiliate structure is beside the point.

The decline in viewership and the shift in advertising spend should be all you need to plan for a next generation news product that behaves much differently than the current model.

It's why creating a next generation news product will benefit your news outlet regardless of whether the affiliate structure survives as is.

Either way, failing to create a next generation news product will assure you of a lonely future.

Redefine Innovation

On its best day television news is suicidal.

Why?

Because it routinely sacrifices long-term rewards for short-term or immediate gains. We behave no better than the companies we criticize for making the quarterly numbers at the expense of longer-term returns.

We are high frequency traders who are slaves to pennies rather than Warren Buffet who earns dollars over the long-term.

The long-term investments television stations should be making in regard to building what author Seth Godin defines as a tribe, enterprise content creation and innovative distribution of that content, are often neglected in favor of near- term goals and achievements.

The industry has taken what should be its long-term ambitions and compressed them into quarters. Blame it on growing corporate ownership, an outdated sweeps mentality, or internal benchmarks we've pledged to meet. Whatever the reason, television news has become shortsighted and, in turn, has damaged its ability to innovate.

Innovation requires a long-term mentality.

That's not to say innovators aren't in a hurry.

Or that innovation cannot happen quickly.

Or that innovators don't want to create the next big thing tomorrow.

However, successful innovators realize that building something that creates value for themselves and others generally takes time.

A lot of time.

Facebook and Twitter were created over a number of years and they're still not finished.

They are projects.

Imperfect and incomplete.

Yet getting better little by little.

What sorts of yardsticks do you think these company founders used to identify whether progress was being made? The next sweeps period? Three months? The next book? Did they throw out their July numbers since summer is the excuse we use for not engaging with as many people as we'd like?

Television news is playing for the next book rather than the next generation.

That's why the industry is suicidal.

On its best day.

When is the last time your newsroom innovated? Below are several "innovations" news bosses have heaped praise upon over the years:

- A new graphics package
- Lower thirds that move
- Full screen graphics that include natural sound
- A brand new set that sparkles more than a competitor's
- A new weather package
- A website redesign
- Lights beneath the set that brighten an anchor's neckline
- Focus group research that dictates story selection
- Anchoring from the field
- A redesigned newsroom
- Broadcasting tweets and Facebook posts

Each of these may have a place in a newsroom or newscast. Each might even positively impact the final product in some way. But none consistently or routinely provide a material impact on newscast quality, viewership ratings, or the overall relevance of television news.

These incremental changes, additions, or subtractions are not innovations. At least not true innovation.

None of these would be granted a patent.

There is nothing proprietary about any of the above.

Please don't misunderstand. I'm not arguing that these things are not at least somewhat important to a newscast. But these are tweaks to be made after you've begun creating and distributing a quality product. One that's in high demand. One that is scarce. One that has others copying you.

The minor tweaks I describe should count as nothing more than bows on top of an already fantastic present.

If you mistake these for true innovation you've traded the horizon for the quarter.

You've allowed yourself to be brainwashed.

I'm urging you to set your sites on true innovation. Something revolutionary. Something that alters the course of broadcast news.

Unfortunately, television news has to go way back to identify true innovation:

- Signal strength improvements
- Microwave shots
- Satellite trucks
- Live war reporting
- The ability to stream

These are all technological advances.

However, it's the bootstrap mentality we no longer possess for which I'm most concerned.

We've become an industry of copycats.

Brainwashed drones relying on the same consultants, the same set-builders, and the same baritone voices to punctuate carbon copy promotions nationwide.

We ought to be ashamed.

We've traded our individuality, inventiveness, and ingenuity to follow the same program our peers and competitors follow.

In fact, we pay outsiders like consultants, set-builders, and analysts to tell us how to fit in. How not to stand out. How to do it like everyone else is doing it.

Commodity news is safe. It's secure. And it's efficient. We've seen it elsewhere which reinforces the idea we are doing it correctly. We've swallowed the Kool-Aid.

And we became fat when we were the only game in town.

Rather than continuing to reinvent the wheel, tweak the way we tell stories, and force the anchors to interact a bit more, we must engage in authentic innovation.

Look at some of the most successful companies of our day- Apple, Amazon, eBay. Each of them reinvented how we accomplish a certain chore:

- How and why we use a phone
- How and when we buy books
- Where and how we pay for goods

Steve Jobs was obsessed with creating something that was highly functional yet elegantly designed. He wanted to surprise people with something even they could not imagine. This is why he didn't routinely use focus groups. Otherwise, the iPhone would not have been invented when and how it was.

Jobs' distribution also broke the box. "Oh yeah, there's one more thing…" Simply uttering those words meant something big was about to be unveiled.

When is the last time you truly surprised someone with your newscast?

Jeff Bezos is obsessed with Amazon's customers- their wants, needs, and desires. He preaches that if employees will take care of customers then everything else will fall into place. Others preach similar mantras but Bezos lives it.

And he has been correct.

Bezos routinely sacrifices quarterly profit margin to invest in the future. However, investors do not penalize him for quarterly results that, at first blush, appear to be from a company much less successful. Shares of Amazon trade at a multiple much higher than companies that are simply trying to make the quarterly numbers.

When you think of eBay what comes to mind?

Yes, that's where you sell the Christmas gift you don't really want.

But it's much more.

Not only did eBay disrupt the online retail marketplace it also changed how people pay for those goods.

PayPal disrupted the credit card industry and is now being accepted offline at major retailers. In fact, some Wall Street analysts say PayPal is worth as much as eBay itself and argue spinning it off of eBay would unlock even more value.

These are true innovations.

Each solves a problem, makes life easier, or surprises us by providing us with something we hadn't previously imagined on our own.

It's our job to do the same with television news.

Device Agnostic

Television news is what we do.

More importantly, it's who we are. A great number of us in the industry siphon a portion of our identities from the fact we create television.

It's not just a medium.

Our identities are intertwined with the medium.

Time to untangle that mess.

If we are to survive and thrive we must adopt new identities. Identities that are much more malleable than those we've assumed in the past. Those of us still referring to television as the business we are in are doomed to follow our newscasts into the grave of irrelevance. Those of us still believing that television is what we do, how we make our livings, and on what we base a portion of our worth must change our mindset.

If you had to pick one device today to hang your hat on I doubt many of you would pick the television.

Or at least the television as we know it.

At least in the near-term.

Television is static.

Beautiful but static. It lacks the transactional nature of other devices which attract more affluent and younger audiences.

At least for now.

However, I argue the television will soon change. And that change will play a key role in how we construct future newscasts. In fact, it'll require us as broadcasters to innovate faster than the Apples, Amazons, and eBays of the world.

We must move quicker in building our newscasts than the inventors who are creating the hardware by which our newscasts will be consumed.

We are, by default, tethered to a stationary device rather than one millions of people carry in their pockets.

Before I explain how you too can innovate faster than Apple when it comes to building a newscast, we have to start over.

We must remove the bias we have for television.

It means we must divorce the one with whom we fell in love and invite a myriad of others into our love lives. We must become hardware polygamists.

Put another way, we must become device agnostic.

As content creators it is no longer our job to choose where, how, or when our content is consumed. The fact that we enjoyed that luxury for so long is exactly why we are in the mess we are in today. Controlling exactly how people consume our content is an addiction none of us want to give up. But it is an addiction we must break if we are to be relevant in the future.

The resistance we've put up has cost us viewers and made us impractical and irrelevant to a generation of digital natives.

Smartphone, dumbphone, tablet, or Google Glass we must eliminate the bias we have for the hardware that attracted us to the business and embrace the choice consumers now take for granted.

We must also build a next generation news product that is adaptable to an array of operating systems.

Hearst Corp. is anything but agnostic in terms of operating systems. It recently invested in Roku, a set–top box maker that streams internet content to television screens. Roku's CEO Anthony Wood says this is the sweet spot for streaming video.

Smart TV developers will choose which operating system is right for them. Hearst has obviously disclosed its preference. Whether your parent company does the same is a matter of individual choice.

At the very least you'll want a front row seat in the selection process so you can build a next generation news product that leverages the full capabilities of the operating systems that become most popular.

Remaining device agnostic is important in terms of making your product attractive to advertisers. However, a more narrow approach in terms of operating systems is likely to yield results not available to those who take a more hands-off approach.

We shouldn't care how viewers watch us.

Where they watch us.

Or when they watch us.

As long as they're watching us, right?

Wrong- sort of!

While we must begin better catering to those most likely to consume what we create we must also routinely check our language.

Our language tells on us.

Getting an audience to "watch" us is only a portion of the goal.

We must embrace the fact that viewers have become much more than viewers. Gone are the days where we expected them to sit passively and allow us to preach unidirectionally to them.

Rather than persuading an audience to "watch" what we produce we should be offering them an opportunity to engage.

An audience that routinely engages with our content in some manner is an audience that advertisers will perceive as having much more value.

Understand audiences will one day carry valuations, or multiples, just like shares in publicly traded companies garner. Broadcasters will charge advertisers based on each segmented audience's valuation. More on this later when I explain why you must also stop selling advertisements, as we know them, to compliment your reinvented newscast. If you cannot wait to learn why, turn now to page 108.

An engaged audience is one less likely to turn away.

The goal will be to offer a product so rich in content and value, for both the audience and advertisers, that each will get lost in your offering and engage in a manner we never even dreamed of when piping our product through a traditional television.

The $5 Million Question

Why does the 21st richest guy in the world invest $5 million in a website of which the majority of your audience has likely never heard?

Because he sees value being created.

That's why Amazon CEO Jeff Bezos invested $5 million in Henry Blodget's *Business Insider*, a website known best for its slide shows and short news pieces on everything from business to entertainment.

The site isn't yet 6 years old but says it draws approximately 24 million readers a month though that's not consistent with data from comScore.

Either way, Bezos is not likely to invest in just any website. This is the guy who created the Kindle book reader from scratch and disrupted the entire book industry.

Now it appears Bezos sees an opportunity to disrupt traditional media.

Business Insider caters to people working on Wall Street and in technology. Some might call those niche audiences. But I call them high-income audiences.

That's not the only thing that likely caught Bezos' eye though.

Business Insider, according to *Bloomberg*, "…chooses topics based on real time data about what readers are clicking on."

So the site, which is not profitable but generates millions in revenue, makes its decisions based on outcomes rather than opinions. Let this be a lesson to news directors still paying television news consultants to conduct focus groups.

Now compare yourself to *Business Insider*.

Visitors wind up getting lost in the site. Editors are watching in real time and using data to drive decision making.

Now recall how differently your editorial meeting was conducted this morning. There was no real time data. Editorial decisions weren't based on analytics. Nope. It was a group of people sitting around a table, partially distracted by their smartphones, attempting to determine what a mass audience might sample later in the day.

Editorial decisions are often based on hunches about the masses rather than data from a niche.

Sounds rather prehistoric.

But what if disruption found you?

Rather than racking your brain for the next big thing what would happen if the next big thing landed on your desk? Would you embrace it? Would you see it for what it was? Or would you mistake it for something else, possibly a threat?

More importantly, would you take legal action in hopes of killing it?

It's happening.

If you're not well versed on Aereo, a Barry Diller backed company that scoops up over-the-air- broadcast signals and funnels them to smartphones, tablets, and laptops for subscription fees, below is a synopsis, *Sour Digital Grapes*, I first distributed online:

∞

Sour Digital Grapes

Broadcasters are begging people to watch their programs online but have largely failed to achieve their goal in quantities and manners most attractive to advertisers.

Then along comes a company, Aereo, that corrals broadcast networks' over-the-air television signals and resells them to web subscribers.

Instead of attempting to out-innovate the Barry Diller backed Aereo, we first told you _here_ 9 months ago how broadcasters filed suit to stop Diller's efforts.

Now, broadcasters have lost another bid to stop Aereo and are now threatening to pull their content, at least their best, from the public airwaves in an effort to deprive Aereo.

Aereo is accused of stealing content.

In reality the company figured out how to do something broadcasters largely have not- get people to pay online for content they once received for free over the air.

The war on Aereo is sour digital grapes.

Rather than innovate (like Diller) broadcasters file suit.

That said, it's understandable why the non-innovators might sue: Diller is getting for free what cable providers pay broadcasters handsomely for (retransmission fees).

However, the fight broadcasters are waging boils down to the fact they are attempting, "...to preserve an obsolete analog business model in the age of digital ubiquity," according to _The Wall Street Journal_.

Either way, the most valuable asset broadcasters have (arguably) is the spectrum the federal government has granted them. The public would be better served (as evidenced by the decline in television news) if broadcasters could sell (without FCC meddling and returning some of the money to taxpayers) the spectrum to wireless providers who would no doubt use it better than broadcasters.

Decades ago, broadcasters agreed to provide a public service in return for use of Uncle Sam's spectrum.

Estimates vary, but just 1 or 2 in 10 households receive this "public service" exclusively over the air now.

Considering broadcasters' dying business model...

The decline in the quality of television news...

And broadcasters' costly legal challenges of those who outsmart them…

If this is how broadcasters plan to use the spectrum they've been allowed to make fortunes on, then the greater public service would be to expedite the transfer of the spectrum to those who might provide the public with faster connections, better data transmission rates, and clearer smartphone calls.

That, today, would truly be public service.

∞

Sour Digital Grapes may anger many of you. You might argue I don't fully understand the issue. Or the inherent unfairness in what's happening.

Go ahead and be angry.

Pick a fight with Diller. Sue him nine ways to Sunday.

I'd rather spend my time and energy creating a viable alternative for the future.

No matter what you believe about Aereo, you cannot argue the fact that Diller is getting people to do what we as broadcasters are only dreaming of. We can file as many suits as we can fund but they will not yield any additional viewers for us.

Lawsuits, if successful, will reduce the viewers Aereo has.

But that does nothing to ensure that we have a future.

Whether the "incentive" auctions the FCC is engaged in to get broadcasters to pony up their spectrum are complete, fair, or not, is outside the scope of this book. The example is simply included here as a reminder that we have become lazy.

Instead of seizing opportunity, we litigate it.

We must do better.

And we must do it now.

Nick Winkler

How a Doughnut Wrecked Television News

It was the sweet glaze that blinded us.

No one is willing to admit it because nearly everyone involved is partially guilty.

It's the erosion of credibility.

A credibility deficit exists in the United States. We don't trust our lawmakers, our bankers, or each other. Much has been written on the subject but television news has gotten less attention than other entities for which trust, hope, and sincerity are lacking.

It happened sometime ago.

It was our Adam and Eve moment.

There we were in the journalistic Garden of Eden—the newsroom—when all of a sudden there it sat for all to see. It was beautiful. It had an aroma that attracted people from every corner of the newsroom. Best of all, especially for poorly paid overnighters, it was free!

That free doughnut we took was costly.

We've been paying for that first bite ever since.

Reporters don't even think about it. Neither do producers. And unfortunately neither do most news managers. They simply grab the doughnut, sandwich, or candy provided to us for "free".

They mean well- morning show guests, well-wishers, or advertisers who leave these bounties on the assignment desk for all to enjoy.

But each time a newsroom employee partakes they voluntarily trade a bit of their credibility. They put the world on notice they are for sale at a bargain price. They voluntarily give up what separates them from journalistic amateurs.

I suspect most have never given it this much thought.

They're either too busy, too poor, or too ill-equipped mentally to understand what they are giving up, what they are trading when they eat the crumbs left behind by those who aim to influence us.

It is subtle.

And I have faith the majority of those who consume these bounties would still be able to objectively cover those who leave behind breakfast or lunch for us.

However, it's this disregard the bulk of the industry has toward perception that is most disturbing. What would the public think should it learn that journalists routinely take gifts from those they may one day be relied upon to report on critically? Might the public be forgiven if it was to pause and wonder about our integrity?

We're often critical of politicians who fail to disclose gifts or obey other disclosure rules. Why are we different?

We're not.

So we keep it secret.

We don't disclose at the end of each newscast who provided us lunch for the day. We don't always disclose the discount reporters receive on haircuts salons often trade for advertising. We don't always broadcast the discounts anchors receive on suits or dress clothes.

It's no big deal, right?

A cookie here. A doughnut there.

But it's not okay.

The people providing these gifts think we are for sale. The problem is they're right. These perks, whether we are consciously aware or not, accumulate over time. We reinforce the hunch gift givers have each time we accept. And each time we fail to disclose our behavior to the public.

Those providing the gifts are slapping high fives.

It's a successful public relations stunt in their eyes.

But in the eyes of the viewers we claim to represent it's something much different. Ask them. I have. They don't like it.

Why would we give them any reason to distrust us?

If you can think of one and are willing to post it on your website for all to see, please send it to nick@thewinklergroup.net and I will gladly admit I'm wrong, refund the money you paid for this book, and acquiesce to all of you who believe I'm being too hard on the industry.

Jeff Harris would disagree though. He's the standout News Director at KMGH in Denver. While the city's food pantries likely disapprove, Harris routinely picks up food left at his assignment desk and heaves it into trash cans.

It's the principle.

I'm told some of his staffers are bothered by it and, at least initially, think junking food gifts is over the top. I enacted a "use no names" policy for this book. But I made a lone exception in Harris' case because his integrity stands out in a crowd that often compromises its own.

A single doughnut.

That's how it all started. That first juicy bite in the news Garden of Eden has sentenced us to lives of journalistic sin.

Ever since that first doughnut we've been compromising. Hoping we might be able to cover our warts. Rigging a newscast so viewers might not see our staffing weaknesses. Stunting Friday nights so we might juice our ratings and charge advertisers more than what a commercial is worth.

Skeleton weekend crews that attempt to make themselves look bigger than they are in an effort to disguise our apathy toward content on Saturday.

We've been faking it.

But just like a drunk who thinks that little mint is masking a night on the town, we're not really fooling anyone.

No one, that is, besides ourselves.

What we need is a clean slate.

However, clean slates don't come easily.

We must wean ourselves from the addictions that now jeopardize our future.

TV News Rehab

If only it were just a 12-step program.

We've become addicted to so many things that are hurting us, even killing us, we're in need of much more than simply a 12-step program.

We've got to break bad habits. We must unlearn some of the teachings of consultants. We must stop and examine conventional wisdom.

How do we know conventional wisdom is correct?

Why are we so sure the way we are doing things is the best way? Is it because we've seen it done elsewhere? Is it because we were #1 in a past life executing a specific set of tactics or techniques? Is it because a focus group told us that's what it wanted to see? Is it based on experience, gut, or intuition?

Can we even answer these questions honestly?

What's clear is that many television news tactics, techniques, and strategies have been mistaken for industry heirlooms worthy of generational passage. Many have evolved as coping mechanisms or ways to deal with declining ratings, shrinking staffs, or other threats to our livelihood.

We've been brainwashed, misled, and confused. Maybe not intentionally, but it has happened. Rather than fix the limp in our step we've been handed crutches. Lean on these, we're told. But the limp doesn't go away. We cover up. Make due. And get along subpar hoping no one notices.

We've made a beeline for the bottom.

And we've found what we were looking for.

We only have so much further to fall.

Then what?

We need to toss the crutches aside, identify what's causing us to limp, and fix the problem. This will not be easy work. In fact, it may be the most difficult work in which we've ever engaged. It'll require us to admit we have been wrong. Or simply that we are no longer right. It means we'll have to own our mistakes. It means we'll have to take responsibility for the positions in which we find ourselves.

Television news must check itself into rehab.

We've stayed out too late. We've crashed daddy's sports car. And our mug shots have had fun poked at them by late night comedians.

If we are serious about creating value for viewers and advertisers we must also be serious about getting rid of what got us into the predicament we are in. We must break our addictions if we are to reinvent television news.

Scattered over the course of the next several pages are recommendations, anecdotes, and ideas aimed at weaning us from that which is killing us.

It's an 18-step program, in no particular order, and it's just the start.

If you'd prefer to avoid what some might deem a lecture, please jump to page 48 to learn how to be proprietary.

#1 *Quit Sweeps Cold Turkey*

Every day is sweeps so start treating each day as such. News bosses in metered markets tell on themselves when they abide by an outdated sweeps month mindset. What we've told viewers, without words all these years, is that they're not important enough to get our best during the non-sweeps months. Investigations are reserved only for the months when we set our advertising rates. Serious story promotion is reserved for time periods when we know our ratings count. Sweeps months are transparently selfish. Disagree? Then grab a megaphone and shout this at your audience:

"We interrupt our normally scheduled laziness in an attempt to use you. If you'll just hang with us into the next quarter hour we'll be able to soak our advertisers for a few extra bucks. It won't take long, please? We promise to go away for a couple of months and leave you alone. Until then- we're fighting for you/ on your side /in your corner (insert your own branding cliché)!"

Start respecting your audience if you want it to respect you. If you're only giving them your best or trying your hardest four months out of the year, which is now three months for many as they have given up on the July sweep, you cannot expect them to turn to you when you need them. You must prove daily to them that they need you if you want them to be there when you need them.

#2 *Stop Putting the Web Second*

Pushing your stories to the website after your newscast communicates, without words, where your priorities lie. This is not a digital strategy. Neither is copying and pasting Associated Press, or AP copy, to the web and calling yourself a digital player. Just because you host a content-rich website does not mean you are web focused. In fact, for the majority the web is an afterthought. A laborious chore that reporters are forced to engage in after the main event, the traditional televised newscast, has ended. If you're digging your heels in right now and looking for a fight because you have spent a lot of time and money on the web and social then I'll simply point to ratings and demographics. Unless you're an outlier, digital natives are not sampling you. It's not because you haven't invested. It's because you haven't committed. Your priorities are backward. Later, when I show you how to reinvent television news, I'll help you understand how the web will actually funnel people to your traditional newscasts when executed properly. Right now, the majority have it backward. The priority should be web and social first. Television second.

#3 *Google-killing Teases Must Die*

Any tease that might be answered with a Google search before the commercial break ends should never have been conceived, written, or broadcast. I remember exactly where I was sitting on a day off watching my station when I had this epiphany. The anchors spewed a smarmy tease right before the break- the equivalent of, "Ha, ha, ha, I know and you don't...and you'll only find out if you sit through this break..." and I got angry. Why would they do this to me? I immediately hit up Google and before the commercial break had ended I had the answer my co-workers were withholding. My anger was quickly replaced by fear. "Holy cow," I thought, "...this is the end of television news unless we change how we tease." Despite Graeme Newell's superb work and tease writing seminars at *602 Communications*, broadcasters continue to write teases viewers can answer with a smartphone in seconds. Traditional teasing is dead. And that'll be your fate as well if you continue teasing traditionally. This means teasing things like tomorrow's temperature—stop it!

#4 *Require Tickets for Entry into Morning Meetings*

By tickets I mean ideas. Morning meetings, and afternoon editorial meetings for that matter, are depressing gatherings where attention spans the size of gnats preside over the ideas, suggestions, and thoughts of the few who are actually prepared. These people have often been granted the authority to set the day's agenda. The very people most ill-prepared to lead are the gatekeepers. Editorial meetings are chock full of critics and followers. Often, these meetings are light on leadership and ideas. I challenge you to count the number of original, enterprise, or entrepreneurial ideas offered at your next editorial meeting. The kind you haven't heard before- angles, places, or people not previously included in your newscasts. Don't tell your employees you're doing this. Do this for a week. Tally the results and unveil them to the crowd. Then kick everyone out of the meeting with chicken scratch next to their names. Kick everyone lacking an original idea out of the meeting. The people with the ideas now run the meetings. The slackers lose their seats at the table due to their inability to contribute. Only those who have done something to better the day's

32

newscast will be granted a seat at the table. These seats will become coveted. Competition will only serve to increase the quality of the ideas. You'll establish a meeting environment where much is expected- where ideas and data rather than opinion are king or queen. To get in you need an idea not simply a critique. No one lacking an idea should be allowed to trump someone with an idea. Unfortunately that's exactly the case in many newsrooms. Expect more. Demand more. Or replace the laggards with idea generators. It's your future.

#5 *Observe the Spirit of the Law not Just the Letter*
I'm referring to the use of "exclusive" and "breaking" as labels for stories. Stop attempting to inflate your gravitas with false claims. Or semi-true assertions. Or definitions that enable you to not be wrong rather than right. This is black and white. Refuse the temptation to convince yourself there's gray. You can tout these monikers until the cattle come home. You can scream them from the tops of mountains. You're not the one who counts though. It's the audience that'll pass final judgment and it has done so in great numbers. Fires that were extinguished long ago. Interviews that can be seen elsewhere, especially now that they live on indefinitely online. Rather than attempting to convince an audience you're the source for exclusive or breaking news, why not spend your energy proving it? Ultimately, the audience will decide anyway. It never was for you to decide. So stop pressing. And start earning.

#6 *Your Viewers Aren't as Stupid as You Think*
They already know the clichés on which you rely. They already understand those creepy promotions that tell them it's that time of year- sweeps. They already know what

you're likely to include in your rundown (Reporter + Blowing snow = Ratings). They also understand how they are expected to answer focus group questions. Now let's assume I'm wrong. That we must write our stories at a 5th grade level. Let's say these are facts. Even if the audience is comprised of morons, idiots, and intellectual dwarfs we must reconcile their access to information. They have social connections. They live in the information economy. They can check what we say in real time. They can compare all of it with our competitors. If we are appealing to the least common denominator we are ignoring valuable niches. It's an easier path to follow. A path we can take more efficiently than others. But it dead ends.

#7 *Hang Gratuitous Weather Live Shots*
He who wins weather...
I know, I know. Win weather and win the race. Weather is the topic last place stations believe proves that they are actually relevant. Our numbers spike when there's a big weather event. People are turning to us when it counts. That's why we are all over this storm. The people need us. In reality, people have no choice. Let's use a bit of common sense here. When a severe weather situation blankets a market the majority of people hole up in their homes. What else are they going to do besides watch you? They play drinking games. The winner, or loser, guesses how many times the live reporter will wince in pain after being pelted with hail, blowing rain, or debris from a tornado. Not once has a news boss set aside his or her arrogance and considered whether ratings spike during weather events because businesses shut down, roads become impassable, or vehicles might be damaged were one to venture out. Often,

satellite television signals are lost. People are trapped inside
their homes. If they have electricity they tune in because
they want to know when the storm will pass. When their
neighbors might regain electricity. Or whether they may lose
it later in the evening. They're not turning to us because they
want to. They're turning to us because they have nothing
better to do. Or because they feel they have to. If you doubt
what I say then please explain the dramatic decline in
ratings following severe weather. Why is there little or no
residual effect? Why don't viewers stay? Could it be because
they were forced to sample? We need to get over ourselves
and balance our weather perceptions with reality. Not all
ratings spikes are created equal.

#8 *The March Toward Homogeny*
Everyone else led with, fill in the blank, why didn't you? The
question is only pertinent if we agree the subject was a
substantial news event and merited priority. Otherwise, the
tongue lashings executive producers receive for being the
only station in the market to lead with something original is
counterproductive. The fear that permeates newsrooms is
often thick. Unfortunately it's also anticompetitive as it
creates incentives to produce carbon copy newscasts that
lack differentiation. If your newscast lacks content that
differentiates it from competitors you are intentionally
blending in with those around you. Ask your advertisers
how they feel about that. Homogeny is the enemy. But
newsrooms across the country embrace it as if it was safe. As
if it provided job security. It's the herd mentality that
believes there is safety in numbers. In reality, running with
the pack erodes job security and safety over the long-term.
Many consultants, news directors, and newsroom managers

have adopted a one-size-fits all-strategy. Once they identify something that works for one reporter they falsely believe it's time to scale that attribute. They believe each reporter on staff should adopt the attribute or skill. We train reporters to perform like others despite inherent differences. If it works for one it must work for the other. Copy. Paste. It's part of the commodity news mentality. It's part of the march toward homogeny. Instead, smart newsrooms embrace the inherent strength in diversity. Smart news bosses will identify individual strengths and then exploit them. Don't misunderstand or perceive I'm asking you to ignore weaknesses. Continual self-improvement and lifelong learning are attitudes reporters must come equipped with. Weaknesses are to be improved upon. Reporters are often given detailed performance scripts and told to follow them regardless of their strengths or weaknesses. If the consultants are effective the reporters they coach begin to walk, talk, and act alike. A staff of zombie reporter drones is created. And then news bosses wonder why their newscasts fail to attract discerning viewers. Those with distinctive tastes, preferences, and desires—high-income earners. There is a great divide between shoring up weaknesses and embracing individuality. Exploiting strengths is much more time consuming for a news boss. It requires a keen eye. It requires an investment. It means you must truly understand what motivates that employee. It's much more efficient to develop a plan and ask each reporter to execute the plan. It's much more comfortable to do that than it is to mold the plan around the individual strengths of your staff members. It's much easier to continue the march toward homogeny.

#9 *Clowns on Cocaine (Stop rewarding them)*

You know who you are. The consulting group that ginned up focus group data on reporter involved live shots and pawned it off as valid and reliable. Yep, you know who you are and you ought to be embarrassed. So should the news bosses who have taken this advice hook, line, and sinker. Newsrooms nationwide require their reporters to bounce around on live shots like clowns hopped up on cocaine: overly animated facial expressions, wild gesticulation, the walk and talk to nowhere. Oh, let's not forget my personal favorite- pulling on the door handle of a locked government building during a 10 P.M. live shot. The walk to nowhere is laughable. In fact, viewers make fun of and are turned off by overly emphatic reporters. It might actually work for some reporters- for the few who can pull it off naturally. For those whose personalities are predisposed to behaving emphatically. But it's wrong for the majority. It has not proven to increase ratings. In fact, I challenge any news director reading this to find one viewer who'll tell you, "I'm tuning in tonight to see how Reporter X moves around on her live shot." Find me just one and I'll buy up every copy of this book, donate all the profits to your newsroom, and burn the pile of books on the front lawn of your station. In reality, viewers are not even aware of whether a reporter is live unless there is a compelling reason to be live. Generally, there isn't a compelling reason to be live. And since that is the case we force reporters to make up a reason. We require them to make their surroundings more important than they really are. We give the live shot as much or more thought than we give the story. This is the case in many newsrooms. Live shots will, at times, dictate story selection. Reporters who stand still often find themselves in the hot seat or worse.

Reporters who bounce around a live location like a child in an inflatable trampoline room at a county fair are lauded regardless of their story quality. Reporters are hired because of their demo reel montages rather than the 5-minute investigation that provided the public a service. It's live shots gone wild. Reporters willing to expose themselves on a live shot will undoubtedly get the camera pointed at them. The attention from the news bosses may be flattering but the ratings are speaking loud and clear.

#10 *Feigned Anchor Sincerity*

"Your face could get stuck permanently that way."

-Your Mother

#11 *Watch Us or Your Children May Die*

These are the sweeps month promotions that aim to scare viewers into watching our newscasts. At times they may actually achieve their objective. The problem is they are disingenuous and insincere. And they do not build trust or longevity. If there were truly threats lurking on the viewers' bedspreads, inside their refrigerators, or on the handles of their grocery shopping carts why would newsrooms wait to tell viewers? If there was something dangerous lurking in a baby's crib why withhold that information? Why make viewers wait several days? Isn't telling them immediately the right thing to do? Isn't that how we would want to be treated? Isn't that what we would expect of a trusted confidant? If that's what you want to become then you need to change how your newsroom is teasing sweeps pieces. People want to be scared on Halloween not when they're considering which news program to watch. Scaring viewers into watching your newscast may provide a bump in the

ratings but it lacks staying power. Especially when the threats are overhyped. When a promotion exaggerates a threat it reduces the newsroom's credibility. I realize many of the news directors reading are likely seething right now. You don't oversee the promotions department. That's out of your control. Sorry, but a bit of tough love is in order. You had better make promotions your business. We all know it's often the promo that lands us in legal trouble rather than the story. However, a greater concern is the damage an exaggerated scary tease can do to your brand's integrity. Make promotions your business and make them smarter.
If you insist on a race to the bottom...
If you aim for the lowest common denominator...
If you punch below the belt...
You'll most certainly find what you're looking for.

#12 *Withholding News*

In April 2013 RTDNA ran an article about when newsrooms should withhold news, which mediums are best suited to break certain types of stories, and how to determine whether to break news online or on the air. Memorize the link below and type it into your web browser to read the whole thing:
https://www.rtdna.org/article/when_newsrooms_withhold_news
While the article's author, Ben Mercer, says he's heavily in favor of breaking news online, the illustration he sites is transparently selfish and incomplete.
While I applaud Mr. Mercer for including newsworthiness as a criterion, the other two he cites (ratings & virality) out his newsroom's true colors- selfish and lacking a viewer-centric mentality. Ratings and virality must be replaced with what's best for the viewer. Remember Amazon CEO Jeff

Resurrecting TV News

Bezos' idea that if you take care of the customer everything else will take care of itself? Well this holds true for television news ratings and digital virality. When web and television mangers disagree about where to break news Mercer writes, "...I'll often plan to post it online, but not until about 8 p.m., when I know the other stations can't catch up." I understand it. I've even been guilty myself. But doing so is wrong. If we are truly focused on our viewers rather than ourselves and our competitors then we will break news via every medium possible and as soon as we possibly can. If you want to see how being selfless and breaking news online and during off hours will actually push viewers to your traditional newscast, jump ahead to page 65. There is a cumulative effect to breaking news immediately rather than a one-off benefit. Still not convinced? Then run this outdated type of thinking through the Warren Buffet test. Whenever you are at a crossroads or are unsure of how to behave, Buffet says to ask yourself how you'd feel if your actions wound up on the front page of *The Wall Street Journal*. Would you be embarrassed? Would your mother call and yell at you? Would your viewers distrust you? Okay, let's try it. Several potential headlines are below:

- News Station Withholds News to Spite Competitors
- News Station Keeps News From Viewers in Effort to Spike Ratings & Charge Advertisers More
- News Station Breaks News Online Only Because it May Go Viral & Result in Page View Tidal Wave

How might your viewers feel about these headlines? Of course, the headlines are raw. And brutal. But they are honest representations of what the RTDNA article is advocating. Would you be comfortable with viewers reading these headlines? If so, stay the course and we'll see how it all plays out in good time. But I suspect the majority understand none of the headlines put the viewer first. Which means the debate over withholding news should be put out of its misery for good.

#13 *Viewers Won't Watch or Sit Through Longer Stories*

- 60 Minutes
- Frontline
- Charlie Rose

Three reasons why news bosses are clearly wrong.

The truth about why you're not executing longer form stories is much more abrasive, hurtful, and telling:

- You have no one on staff who can execute an in-depth piece
- You are simply not willing or able to dedicate the necessary resources to execute longer form pieces
- You fear angering a portion of your audience, losing an advertiser, or the criticism that often accompanies investigatory work

News directors are right in one regard: some people will not sit through a longer form piece. One that is complex, nuanced, and contains areas of gray. In an age when newsrooms will take a ratings spike any way they can get it (beggars can't be choosers) I suspect there's little interest in doing anything other than pandering to the masses. However, I would urge news bosses willing to innovate to raise their standards. To be a bit more discerning. I'm saying you should pick your audience. It's backward when compared to the mass appeal strategy currently being employed. I'm urging niche appeal. Niches must not be so narrow in scope that they cannot pay the bills. But creating a product for an audience that appreciates content similar to what *Frontline* produces just might reward you in a manner you had not anticipated. What kind of audience would be more valuable to advertisers? One with the attention span of a gnat? Or one willing to invest in something you've created with them in mind? A piece that can't be consumed in the time it takes to eat a peanut. An audience that appreciates emotional intelligence. How do you think the two audiences I've briefly introduced compare in terms of income? Which do you think advertisers might be partial to?

#14 *Give Your TV News Consultants Raises*

Seriously. They are some of the most talented people on the planet. They are highly skilled persuaders of the finest order. In fact, they have pulled off one of the greatest heists in history. They have gotten news directors, general managers, and corporate media moguls to continue paying them large sums of cash despite lackluster performance. I pray one day I am as convincing as these folks have been. Television news ratings continue to decline yet newsrooms continue to rely on the same outside help. The very people responsible, in part, for the decline in ratings are the same people news bosses continue to pay for advice on how to boost ratings. What other line of work continues to employ consultants who serially fail to change the fortunes of those paying them? Please don't misunderstand my criticism. Television news consultants are extremely intelligent. I envy how easily they talk television stations out of their money. I'm jealous of how they routinely convince newsrooms to invite them back. And I'm in awe of how they've managed to largely avoid accountability. These are extremely skilled people. They just haven't earned their money. It's why you should give them a raise. Right?

#15 *Over promise & Under deliver*

Television news stations are guilty of over promising and under delivering on multiple levels. Understand this is exactly opposite of how the majority of companies run their businesses. The best companies attempt to tamp down expectations so they can exceed them when they release quarterly results. These businesses are quite skilled at managing expectations. The higher they set expectations the more difficult it becomes to exceed those expectations and the more likely it becomes the outfit will fall short and miss expectations. It's why Investor Relations, or IR departments, work hard to manage the expectation game. Don't confuse this with intentionally setting the bar low. Organizations that intentionally set expectations too low, just so they can beat them without working hard, are often penalized worse than companies that fail to exceed high expectations. But television news, remember it's suicidal on its best day, routinely elevates expectations in a manner that nearly guarantees it'll not be able to meet or exceed them. We promise the world in our promotions. Our anchor lead-ins oversell the story to come. The majority of topical teases or newscast previews might lead one to routinely believe the world is coming to an end on the same day we've found a cure for cancer again. Our grandiose teases often leave viewers feeling as if they have been shortchanged. As if they had been fooled into sticking around for a story that simply didn't live up to the hype. Viewers who are routinely made to feel this way quickly learn: fool me once shame on you, fool me twice shame on me. If you must tease do so responsibly. Otherwise we should mandate warning labels like the FDA requires of prescription drugs. We could list the side effects associated with outlandish teases:

- Could cause confusion followed by bouts of anger
- May prompt euphoria followed by immense disappointment
- May lead to arthritis in finger used to change channel on remote control

Or we might institute brief messages at the end of the tease much like we require of presidential candidates for accountability purposes:

- I'm (fill in name of News Director) and I approved this outlandish tease

Stop teasing altogether in the traditional sense or do so responsibly if you must. Just as you know you should not drink and drive neither should you over promise and under deliver.

#16 *Fire all of Your Producers*
Not because no one grows up saying, "I want to be a television newscast producer." Not because the majority wanted to be reporters but failed for one reason or another. And not because the majority show up at the morning editorial meeting having not read the morning newspaper

and without a single original idea for the day ahead. Nope, I advocate firing producers because most newsrooms do not allow them, even the competent ones, any creative control over the newscasts they oversee. Newscast producers are often treated as replaceable cogs in place simply to stack shows rather than produce shows that create value for viewers. Newsrooms pay producers next to nothing. But even that is too much for what the majority of stations allow their producers to do. In fact, newsrooms would be better off replacing producers with software that can write copy and stack shows. Narrative Sciences makes software which its creators predict will soon win a Pulitzer Prize. Software doesn't take lunch breaks or call in sick. After the initial investment, software will produce a better return than newsrooms currently allow most producers to engineer. Executive producers generally micromanage producers in a manner that makes them expendable and inconsequential. The choice is rather clear: hire smart creators to produce newscasts with a singular focus on viewers or get rid of them all and allow EPs to plug in the inputs and let the software do its job. Restore the humanity to producing and you may see it bleed through your newscast and connect.

#17 *Get Off the Fence- Stand for Something*
I challenge you to count the number of times you hear these words in your newscasts:

- May
- Might
- Could

These words were ones to be avoided a generation ago. Write one of these words and a crusty editor was likely to force you to do more work to make the piece more definitive. Today though, these words are accepted without second thoughts. They are overused and often attract little or no afterthought. They have replaced hard work. They are a substitute for rigor. They are a lazy reporter's crutch. While I realize these words have a place in newscasts with integrity, they have wrongly become commonplace and often go unquestioned by newsroom managers. News writing guru Mervin Block explains this matter much more eloquently, coherently, and persuasively than I can. Please visit his site to learn more www.mervinblock.com. I also urge you to make his book, *Writing Broadcast News Shorter, Sharper, Stronger,* a must read each year with a written test to follow, for anyone calling your newsroom home.

#18 *Stop Stunting (Stealing from Advertisers)*

It's a dirty little secret your advertisers would not likely forgive- stunting. Stunting, for those who need a refresher, is when stations pull some type of "stunt" so a particular show or portion of a show is not counted in a sweeps ratings period. As you might guess stations do not stunt shows on nights that historically rate highly—think spectacular lead-in program. Nope, stations stunt so historically poor ratings nights, like Fridays, are not counted against them when the ratings are averaged into a composite score. For instance, stations routinely stunt the final 15 minutes of their late Friday night newscasts. They label it as something other than an ordinary newscast, a special, so that chunk of the newscast, which is poorly rated, is not counted against them. *The Nielsen Company,* which tallies television station ratings, is a co-conspirator in this crime. And a crime is exactly what this is. Automobile dealers and furniture sellers beware: television stations are stealing from their advertisers. Stunting skews newscast ratings. It dishonestly inflates viewership ratings and leads advertisers to believe a newscast has more viewers than it actually does. Initially, I planned to write an entire book about stunting entitled: *Screwed! How Television Stations Cheat Advertisers.* I still might. Okay, news directors offended by this, answer one question: How might you feel if you bought a car because it came equipped with 300 horse power only to learn later it had 250? Let's say you also found out the dealer knew the truth but didn't tell you. You'd be angry. You'd feel the dealership had been less than truthful with you. You'd want some of your money back. Why? Because you did not get all that you paid for. Advertisers should feel the same. Television stations should refund the money they've stolen from advertisers. Imagine if every entity that had ever purchased a television newscast advertisement was certified as a class and allowed to file a class action lawsuit. The award might bankrupt television stations that routinely stunt. The bottom line is you wouldn't want to be treated like this by outfits with which you do business. So why are you treating your advertisers like this? It's not the advertisers' fault your viewership ratings are down. Disguising a portion of your newscast's ratings decline is deceptive at best and illegal at worst.

Choose to be Proprietary

L ittle of what we produce is actually proprietary. Newsrooms market themselves as proprietary. They tell viewers they are different. They attempt to create an aura of scarcity.

But if we are honest with ourselves the majority of the newsrooms trying to compete today are simply content aggregators. They search for, subscribe to, or otherwise assemble and distribute content produced by someone else.

They market the content as if they were the content originators.

Yes, newsrooms do produce content- daily turn stories, investigations, and consumer pieces. However, even "original content" is increasingly more reliant on content creators outside our own newsrooms. Rather than produce more original content ourselves it has become quicker and cheaper to increase marketing spend. Branding often trumps enterprise reporting and content origination.

Marketing is easier. It can cover our blemishes and warts. But it lacks the longevity truly original content provides.

The problem with becoming aggregators is there is nothing proprietary about that. Anyone with a web connection can become an aggregator. And anyone can do so without the overhead and operating costs of a television station. Siphon off enough eyeballs (which far too many mistake for outcomes), generate just enough traffic, and nearly anyone can quickly be in the business of selling advertisements on their website.

A connected world not only leveled the playing field, it tilted the balance newsrooms once enjoyed. Newsrooms were once proprietary. Not necessarily by choice, though some were. But today the technology that has grown up around newsrooms has rendered many a commodity. Commodities, unless they're in short supply, do not fetch premium prices. Commodities are undifferentiated products lacking qualitative differentiation across markets.

For those of you who disagree, are angry, or unwilling to honestly consider whether you run a commodity newsroom, I ask that you think back to the Boston marathon bombings. What were your priorities that day?

The bombs exploded midafternoon.

Most newsrooms scrambled to reorganize their rundowns as they should. They began checking the marathon database for local runners. They reached out to local marathon organizers. They asked law enforcement what type of security is in place at local marathons. Newsrooms, on average, did much of what they should have done.

But there was nothing proprietary about what they did.

There was nothing special.

Even newsrooms lucky enough to have marathon-running anchors in Boston during the bombing did nothing to stand out from thousands of other aggregators.

Now compare your newsroom's priorities with those of Google.

I can already hear you interrupting. You're ready to argue that my comparison is flawed. It's not apples to apples. That Google is simply an aggregator of everyone else's content as well.

All of those points are well taken.

But while newsrooms across the country were frenetically working to copy and paste Associate Press content into their rundowns as if it were their own...

As newsrooms hurried to record phone interviews with marathon runners from their local markets, many of whom were nowhere near the blast site...

While newsrooms inadvertently began blending in with the media crowd around them...

Google was creating value for its audience.

It was providing a public service that would create lasting bonds with its audience.

It was building the kind of trust no marketer can.

Amid the chaos, Google was helping to reconnect those separated from their loved ones during a time where cell service was spotty. It's called Google Person Finder and it enables anyone to be a conduit between those who become separated from one another by crisis or tragedy. It helps people connect when cell phone service is cut, like it was as a precaution initially in Boston to prevent any additional bombs from being detonated. In a nutshell, Google provides a proprietary service to anyone wanting to let the world know they are searching for someone after a crisis. It enables friends, families, and loved ones to reconnect during the worst of times.

But Google doesn't hoard this service.

Nope.

It gives Person Finder to anyone who'd like to use it.

It is a gift.

Google shows anyone interested how to embed Person Finder in their own website. It provides the skeletal backbone for any entity truly wishing to connect with its viewers in a time of need.

Several newsrooms appeared to have at least told viewers that Google offered a service that essentially created a database for the missing. But widespread adoption was not apparent.

Rather than marketing to viewers your newsroom is "On Your Side"…

Rather than attempting to persuade viewers you provide, "Coverage You Can Count On"…

Why not show them?

Why not be the station that tells viewers with loved ones in Boston that this is the channel to which they can turn if they are trying to find a loved one? Why not at least be a conduit between your audience and those from whom they have been separated?

I've witnessed firsthand how newsrooms cede opportunity to outsiders. Someone not even on the competitive radar.

It wasn't a television station but rather a lone wolf who provided value to those afflicted by a tornado that destroyed parts of North Minneapolis in 2011.

A New Yorker with ties to North Minneapolis started a Facebook page immediately after the tornado struck. It quickly became the place victims, their loved ones, and even the traditional media went to learn what was happening in their community.

One person sitting in an apartment thousands of miles away created the conduit necessary to connect victims with help. This page connected victims with food, toiletries, and temporary housing. It empowered a community to find those who needed their roofs tarped before the next rain. It reunited victims with beloved pets they thought had been lost. And it allowed mothers to find diapers, dry socks, and hot meals for their now homeless children.

One person.

One Facebook page.

Thousands of miles away from the disaster.

The majority still reading are likely ready to pounce on my logic. You're ready to poke holes in my reasoning. You're ready to dig your heels in.

The code Google provides to users…

The free Facebook page…

Neither of those would specifically count as proprietary technology for a newsroom smart enough to grasp and leverage them.

However, when I refer to proprietary I'm not implying you need to invent the next patentable semiconductor innovation. I'm not arguing you must employ an army of creators to generate troves of intellectual property. I'm not saying you've got to create something from scratch in your Austin garage or your California dorm room.

I'm arguing you must adopt a proprietary state of mind. One that is always hunting new ways to make connections. To earn the permission of an audience. A mindset that tenaciously seeks out the trust of an audience.

These aren't objectives that may be achieved with commodity newscasts.

Or transparently selfish marketing.

These objectives are only to be achieved by those with an authentic desire to serve their tribes.

If the goal is to boost viewership…

Or push viewers to the web…

Or keep them through the break…

You are doomed to a hellish eternity of ratings decline.

If however, you adopt a service-minded approach, one that puts the needs of your viewers before your own…

One that shows them you're willing to use your energy, your resources, or those provided for free by others to benefit them in some manner...

These are the newsrooms that are exhibiting proprietary characteristics. These are the newsrooms that stand out when others are working hard to blend in. Adopting an outside-in approach is what we were meant to do when we were entrusted with the people's spectrum.

Only after we dedicate our minds to being proprietary can we actually become proprietary.

Ultimately, newsrooms must become proprietary:

- In technology
- In content
- In delivery

Before I show you how to execute on all three your newsroom will first have to commit to change. It must genuinely be disgusted with being a commodity. In fact, it must be embarrassed by what it has become.

Those who are content with what they are doing...

Those who believe they are truly making a difference cutting and pasting AP copy into the rundown...

Those who are certain they are committed to the web though they only post stories after they've been broadcast on television...

They may be fine people.

They may even be good employees.

But they are not proprietary newsroom employees.

They lack the mindset that will prevent your newsroom from blending in, merging, and becoming just another entity awaiting aggregation.

If that's good enough because you're still making money from commercials, please read no further.

For those who want more- let's go!

Sell Your Tower for Scrap

The steel it is made of may be worth more as scrap than as a broadcast signal distribution tool in the future. Your flame thrower is now tossing the equivalent of embers.

Before we reinvent how we create and distribute our newscasts we have to put some skin in the game of the future. We must consider what the world might look like years from now.

That's what the device makers are doing.

So we must be looking ahead even farther while still respecting the incremental advances in technology between now and then.

We must at least consider the notion that television as we know it may one day no longer be broadcast in a traditional sense.

We must consider the possibility our broadcast towers will become relics better off as museum pieces rather than connectivity links to those we wish to engage. We must entertain the possibility that what we now call television may one day be viewed via the web entirely. A debate over how this may also jeopardize cable providers is outside the scope of this book.

However, the threat is real.

Those who doubt this need to look no further than Dish's offer to acquire Sprint.

New homes are being built to accommodate a future similar to the one I describe. Televisions as we know them will be mounted to walls with built in web connectivity or the ability to sync with and be controlled by other devices.

The future is closer than you might suspect.

The Google+ Hangouts On Air tool gives everyone the power to be in the "television" business. Not only does it give people the ability to stream to an audience in your local DMA, but On Air also gives them the ability to, "broadcast to the world".

Google's brief description of On Air reads, "Go live in front of a global audience, whether you're an aspiring artist, a global celebrity, or a concerned citizen." The tool, which anyone can use for free, also gives one the ability to stream live.

Additionally, viewers can pause and rewind live streams in real time. They're also available for replay immediately after streams conclude.

Is this a broadcast signal tower killer?

Does this make live trucks irrelevant?

Maybe not immediately but the foundation is being laid quickly.

Imagine what might happen if a group of enterprising reporters, disappointed in the direction local news has taken, were to combine technologies and available fundraising platforms to compete against your television station.

What's stopping the top reporters in your market from quitting their respective stations...

Pooling their talent, sources, and storytelling capabilities...

And using On Air as a basis to compete against the stodgy television stations for which they used to work?

What if they leveraged their notoriety and influence on Kickstarter, a marquee crowdfunding platform, to raise money for their newsgathering operations? What if they crowdfunded stories important to slivers of your market? What if they offered your sales department money to advertise their news product during your newscast?

Should they generate enough traffic Google itself would pay them a portion of the advertising revenue they helped earn.

I'm certain many of you are shaking your head in disbelief. The picture quality is lacking as might the ability to stream live from more remote locations.

I'm not arguing those points.

The platform that might ultimately make competition like I describe a reality may not be ready for prime time just yet.

But the ingredients are there.

The technology is improving. The discouraged reporters who still have the bug are in each market. And a means to fund such an operation are in place.

Your broadcast tower may not be scrap yet. But it's certainly losing some of its value.

It all means we'll be required to fundamentally change how we perceive our place in the world. More specifically, we will no longer be limited by time or space.

Right now we are slaves to time and space.

We back time our newscasts so we hit commercial breaks at precise times. We trim or stretch our newscasts so we're off the air in time for the next show to start. We fit what we can into the allotted space. At times we have wiggle room. On other days we have more content than will fit in the allotted space and time.

However, the time and space slaves of the past are being set free.

We are being emancipated.

It's not Lincoln, it's the web!

But what are people once enslaved by time and space to do with their newfound freedom? Former slaves must acclimate themselves to their new world. One that will be free of precisely timed advertisements, hard breaks, and network requirements to end their shows at the bottom of the hour.

We are experiencing a time and space glut.

We are not likely to run out of either in the future. We can use or take up as much or as little as we want. The opportunity this creates is immense. The flexibility this gives us is unique.

No longer must we stretch content that ought not to be stretched. Never again must we cut something of importance due to time constraints.

The web provides us the canvas we've always desired. One we can shrink or elongate as we please. One that is malleable rather than rigid. One that we can change every day, intraday, and again tomorrow.

In real time.

The canvas of the future is similar to an accordion.

It's up to us to learn to play it harmoniously.

The freedom from time and space constraints carries with it the potential to impact the future of television news in a manner greater than any other. That's not to say we won't run a traditional 22-minute newscast in some form or fashion in the future. However, it does mean we must not continue to abide by traditional rules based on the constraints of time and space.

Time and space have lost their scarcity online.

Resurrecting TV News

We must not carry the strict rules of broadcast television into a future void of the foundation on which those rules were originally made. Simply put we must adapt our newscasts to the realities brought about by the freedom from space and time:

- Newscasts need not be timed
- Newscasts need not be scheduled
- Newscasts need not routine advertising holes
- Newscasts need not be structured based on quarter hours

This freedom from time and space will also impact how your reporters package news or if they package it at all in certain instances. Of course I'm referring to story length and when a story is made available for consumption.

Note: this isn't a free pass to do 98 hour packages and 15 second burst newscasts.

And please note my word choice above—consumption.

Traditionally, television stations have fed their viewers news. We cooked what we wanted to cook. Served it at the time we wanted to serve it. And those who showed up late for dinner were not able to eat.

Technology has altered the model to a degree. People who show up late can reheat our newscasts online and pick at the leftovers. And stations routinely use focus groups to find out what people want to eat despite the fact they often choose not to eat what we've prepared at their request.

In reality though, we are still attempting to feed viewers.

The problem is we no longer have that authority.

Technology has stripped us of the ability to force feed people. It's why we should choose our words carefully.

There is a sharp distinction between feeding and consuming. Each of the words reflect where the power lies. If we ignore or cannot comprehend to whom the power belongs we are destined for the graveyard. We owe it to ourselves not only to see the distinction but to respect it.

It's our obligation to allow viewers to choose.

Now, if you're beginning to believe I'm simply advocating building a website and calling yourself a news outlet please go back to the beginning of this section and read what I said about respecting incremental advances in technology on our way to wholly consuming television online.

The beginning of the transformation I describe is one in which your competitors should be coming into focus by now.

Do you see them?

I'm sure you think you do. The other affiliates in town. The local newspapers. If that's what you have deemed as your competition I would argue, at least initially, you are mistaken.

In fact, your current affiliate competitors won't be competitors at all if you reinvent your station in a manner similar to that which I am describing. You'll create and distribute so disruptively you'll look nothing like your present day competitors. In fact, your present day competitors won't become competitors again until long after you've reinvented yourself. Only after they witness the fruits of your labor will they too make a similar transformation. By then you'll already be on to new projects, inventions, and innovations that will differentiate you even further from the copycats long behind you.

In fact, once you realize the opportunities that exist when time and space constraints are eliminated you'll understand who your competitors really are.

While you are no longer limited by time your viewers are. Their time is finite.

And you are fighting for a share.

So too will everyone else online. The time and space issue will also redefine how we perceive local markets. *Nielsen* may count just 210 television markets (God bless Glendive!) but the consumer knows better.

An always connected world means a Brazilian YouTube video producer is now your competitor. So too is the Russian blogger highlighting Putin's latest attempt to tamp down protests. If they are in your niche they are your competitor regardless of where they are physically located.

You get the point.

It's not a 4-horse race in your hometown market once you reinvent yourself. It's a mad scramble playing out worldwide.

It means that tower out back has seen its finest days.

Casts are for Broken Bones

Not news.

At least not anymore.

Casts are stiff. They're awkward. They limit our range of motion. That's why when a doctor finally cuts them off we throw them away.

They are trash.

We tell on ourselves when we reinvent the way we create and distribute news but still insist on calling it a newscast. We're clinging to convention rather than fully embracing the change we must undergo.

If you've read this far then I'm betting you're at least considering whether you ought to cut your cast and dump it in the garbage bin.

It's time to get rid of the cast.

What I'm arguing we must create is anything but a cast. Eventually it will not likely even be broadcast. Nor will it be rigid, stiff, or permanent.

Instead it'll be fluid, transactional, and never complete.

In fact, your news will never end.

It will never be finished.

And it will never be over.

That is if you implement at least a portion of the change I'm advocating.

There'll most likely be breathers. Or breaks between the distribution of content. But there will certainly no longer be well-defined beginnings, commercial breaks, and ends as we know them today.

Your news will never be done.

It's constant. It is a work in progress. Something you will continually build upon, improve, change, correct, subtract from, add to, and nudge one way or another.

This is really going to make it much more difficult to apply for all of the awards that reinforce and amplify the egos present in newsrooms!

This work in progress mentality is what must replace the cast mentality we currently hold dear. The one that is familiar, safe, and efficient to reconstruct day after day. There's nothing inherently wrong with the cast. It just simply wasn't designed with the future's technology in mind.

So why would we force a bygone structure upon an audience in a context for which it was not designed?

What you replace your cast with semantically is of little consequence for the purpose of this book. I'm simply concerned with the cast mentality and getting rid of it.

Admittedly, it hurts a bit to advocate this.

I fell in love with the cast as a child. The same time and place every night. I had a standing appointment with Tom Brokaw.

We were booked.

And we were buddies in my mind.

But the digital natives will have grown up with no regard for time or space in terms of newscasts. Right, wrong, or indifferent digital natives will not allow someone with a cast mentality to call the shots. To demand where and when they must show up.

Nope.

They call the shots.

It's up to us to go to them.

It's our responsibility to make them our buddies just like Mr. Brokaw made me his.

Pray You're Molested

Your next generation news product will be molested. It'll be told what to do. And it may even be worn and abused by your viewers.

And this is if you're lucky!

This is how viewers, if you're fortunate enough to have them, will engage with your news product. The news product of the future must be created with multiple consumption models in mind.

And it must be designed with grace, simplicity, and functionality.

Creating a digital news product with optimal accessibility requires it be designed with a hybrid-like mentality. More specifically, it means you must design your next generation news product so that viewers, or hopefully engagers, can touch, talk to, and wear what you create.

The screens of our lives revolve around touch. Eventually, the large screens in our living rooms will also likely be touch sensitive. But will people be motivated to touch a large living room screen the same way they touch a tablet in their lap? The debate among designers is raging and far from settled.

But since we are device agnostic we must plan for touch. We must incorporate touch technology into the creation of our news product regardless of whether people in their living rooms will be motivated to get up, walk toward their screen, and use a finger to select something to consume.

Touch is just one of the three stool legs though.

We must also build our next generation news product so that it's navigatable via voice. Not only must it respond to vocal commands but it also must be enabled to handle the inevitable: technology that finishes our sentences for us.

It may seem far-fetched right now but Google's search engine evolved to do exactly what I describe in regard to our text. When we begin typing a search query Google often knows the rest of what we are about to type prior to us having to type it. We must anticipate similar technology as advances are made in voice recognition technology.

The anticipatory trifecta is wearability.

Our next generation digital news product must have the capability to be consumed while viewers are wearing the hardware through which our product is distributed. I'm dubbing it ornamental media consumption. The ornaments people adorn themselves with will likely contain the same computing power our desktop machines did just a few years ago.

Hardware makers are designing smart watches so people can consume media on their wrists.

Google Glass, tech analysts say, promises to be a major breakthrough or bust. If it's a breakthrough, how intensely have you thought about optimizing your news product so that it's attractive and consumable from inside the lenses of a pair of glasses?

Or how much thought have you given to using your product to create value for people inside their vehicles?

I'm not advocating you must create a separate news product for each and every piece of innovative hardware to hit the market. I am advocating you design your news product around several major themes clearly gaining momentum. If you'll design your news product based on these themes you'll be in a position to quickly optimize your product for whatever piece of hardware wins out in terms of adoption.

Besides touch, voice, and ornamental engagement next generation news product designers must also be conscientious of the convergence of social, mobile, and cloud. We'll discuss this in greater detail down the road. But these are the themes that must underpin our design.

If we design our news product with these concepts in mind we'll create a competitive advantage for ourselves. Our goal should be to make our product as accessible and as easily consumable as possible. Only after we do this do we earn the opportunity to prove our content is superior to that of our competitors.

Failure remains possible.

All of the work we must do in terms of designing a product that is accessible and consumable does not guarantee success. All it does is afford us a seat at the content table of the future. An opportunity to show the world the content we have created. That content must still be of higher quality than our competitors.

However, we will not likely even be afforded an opportunity to see how our content stacks up unless we invest the time, effort, and creativity to get our product where it needs to be: anywhere media consumers are.

The advertisement above the urinal stall inside a restaurant is an opportunity to show off. It's an opportunity to expose your product to someone who may not be familiar with it. The gentleman using the urinal is a captive audience. How will you engage him?

Pray he molests your news product.

But only after he washes his hands!

Redefine Breaking

Creating a successful next generation news product hinges, in part, on redefining breaking news.

First though, how does television news currently define breaking news?

Anyone?

In case you missed the question: what constitutes breaking news at your station?

Anyone?

Not once have I seen a policy, heard a thorough explanation, or gotten a definitive answer after asking this question. Breaking news is like pornography, right? We'll know it when we see it.

Like much of television news the answer is subjective and open for debate. That's not all bad. But it's certainly not helpful when designing a next generation news product.

In short, most can agree news is breaking if it happens during a news broadcast. The majority would also likely agree news is breaking if it happens in the minutes leading up to a news broadcast.

Here's where the debate splinters though.

How much time is allowed to pass before the "breaking" banner is eliminated from our news broadcasts? How long after news breaks is it considered broken? After the problem that caused it to break is fixed? When the flames are out? Once the highway has been reopened to traffic?

A universally agreed upon definition is lacking in terms of longevity.

Why?

Breaking news generally decays quickly. In the natural it is scarce. That's why it is valuable. Television news managers were quick to recognize this. Urgency sells. It attracts viewers.

Historically, breaking news has been a quick high for television stations. Stick the breaking news needle in the vein and euphoria follows. Breaking news events are gifts from the news gods. They provide a quick boost to ratings and ultimately advertising revenue as long as these breaking events are sold correctly.

The problem is breaking news highs don't last long. They dissipate quickly. Since television stations have become addicted they look for more. But remember, real breaking news is scarce on a relative basis. It's tough to come by. The highs are few and far between.

It's why television news began manufacturing breaking news.

Trouble is manufactured breaking news is not nearly as potent. It doesn't deliver the same high real breaking news does. It's not nearly as scarce and doesn't deliver a comparable spike in ratings.

It's why I asked you to define breaking news at the beginning of this section. Your age will likely determine how you answer.

Over the years the definition of breaking news has been stretched.

More specifically, the types of news broadcasters highlight in newscasts has expanded. As has the length of time broadcasters still consider something to be breaking. Broadening the types of news items and the length of time news items are still considered to be breaking have only served to erode the value and power inherent in authentic breaking news.

Television news managers have transformed a scarce but valuable resource into a manufactured commodity with little intrinsic value.

But that hasn't stopped news stations from attempting to train viewers as if they were Pavlovian dogs. Stations routinely start newscasts with some sort of futuristic jingle signifying breaking news in an attempt to force viewers to pay attention. News managers slap breaking news banners on the lower third of a television screen hoping it will keep viewers from turning away. And stations routinely promise more information before the end of the late newscast or in the morning despite knowing their crews are packing up and leaving so as not to run up too much overtime pay.

The truth is television stations don't even believe their own jingles, lower third banners, or anchor proclamations of breaking news. Or at the very least they're not listening to the reporter on scene.

For instance, I once made it to an apartment fire just in time to ask a firefighter two questions and make the top of a 9 P.M. newscast. No one had been injured. The flames were out. And the cause appeared to be a charcoal grill on a balcony.

This was about as routine and uneventful as apartment fires get.

However, an hour later as the 10 P.M. broadcast was beginning and I was listening to the anchor introduction to my live shot in front of the apartment complex I heard in my IFB, my ear piece, a familiar jingle and one of our anchors saying, "We begin with breaking news tonight…"

What followed was infuriating: the anchors describing in the present tense how the flames were billowing from the apartment complex. How firefighters were rushing to the scene and calling for backup. All of it then topped off with an anchor feigning compassion and asking me on live television if anyone had been hurt.

I had only an instant to make a decision.

Here's what I wanted to say (names have been excluded to protect the guilty):

"Hurt? Who told you someone might have been hurt? In fact, had you listened to the report I filed at 9 P.M. you'd know no one had been injured. But that's beside the point now. I'm extremely concerned you're going blind or having hallucinations. Because there are no flames billowing from the apartments behind me. Nope, those were extinguished hours ago. You ought to be able to see that.

Clearly, the first time you read the script was on air. Nice preparation! Maybe you should cut short your dinner and give a darn about the newscast you're overpaid to anchor."

That's what I wish I had said. What I wanted to say. But I learned my lesson years ago about correcting anchors on live television.

I was actually suspended for correcting an anchor on live television. Was told it should not have happened or I should have done so with a bit more finesse. Correcting anchors on live television hurts the anchor's credibility, I'm told.

I guess reporting inaccurate information has no impact on the station as a whole though?

The point here is to illustrate the absurdity that is breaking news. The 24-hour cable news channels have only made matters worse. In fact, breaking news has been watered down so much it provides little or no high at all.

All of that can change though.

You have the authority to redefine breaking news. To stop manufacturing it as a commodity and transition it back to the scarce but valuable resource it once was. However, it'll require an overhaul in how breaking news is defined.

First though, you must acknowledge, respect, and revere authentic breaking news.

Authentic is the key word.

Not only must it be newsworthy but news mangers must also respect its brevity. While exceptions exist, authentic breaking news generally has a short shelf life. That's what makes it unique, valuable, and attractive.

If you'll respect these truths authentic breaking news will respect you.

Resurrecting TV News

This doesn't mean you're sentenced to a life without much breaking news.

In fact, the contrary is true.

Authentic breaking news happens routinely. In your newsroom. You're just not seeing it because you are looking through an outdated prism.

As you redefine breaking news don't forget how technology has eliminated the time and space constraints of yesteryear. When you get rid of the 5, 6, & 10 P.M. newscast notion of time a whole new world opens up. The news product of the future, unlike today's newscasts, is a stream without an end. When you acknowledge and embrace this you'll see a world chock full of breaking news.

When designing the next generation news product you will quickly learn withholding news is a tactic of a bygone era. It is extinct.

In the future news organizations will have no choice but to push news immediately. It's what websites do now. It's what bloggers do via Twitter. And it's what your operation will do in the future only on a much larger scale.

As soon as a reporter finishes her script- break it. As soon as the piece is done being edited- break it. As soon as a VO/SOT is completed- break it.

Newsrooms routinely break news but not in the traditional sense. Today, newsrooms hide each piece of news they complete. They keep it secret. They withhold it until a predetermined time.

Newsrooms of the present day are taking authentic breaking news and turning it into general news. News managers are corralling breaking news and withholding it from their audience. They are keeping a lid on the news they produce.

Rather than breaking it they hold it.

Instead of leveraging its inherent urgency we allow it to dissipate.

We intentionally cause our breaking news to blend in rather than stand out.

It's actually sad. Today's newsrooms are places breaking news goes to die.

Authentic breaking news is happening right under our noses. We're just too blinded by tradition to see it. Instead, we look for external events we might stretch into breaking news. We look for excuses to use our jingles, lower third banners, and anchor proclamations.

I'm certainly not advocating we stop hunting breaking external news.

I'm simply asking you to start seeing the news you break internally. I'm urging you to treat the news you break as breaking. As soon as you are finished with a piece break it. Don't make your audience wait for it.

Just because you break a piece of news doesn't mean it cannot be used later in your news product or elsewhere in your overall strategy.

If you've already made up your mind breaking news as soon as it's done won't work because it disrupts the sales process or erodes advertising value from your news product please put those worries aside for a bit. We're not there yet. But after I show you how we're going to overhaul our news product I will also outline how news organizations must reinvent how they sell a next generation news product. If you can't wait though, I understand.

Jump ahead to *Connection Selling* on page 108.

But before you go…

Please take a moment and comprehend the option I just offered you. I'm not demanding you read the next paragraph, the next page, or the next section as I ordered them. I'm not demanding you follow the book chronologically.

I respect your freedom to roam.

I respect your freedom to choose.

And I respect the fact you might want to consume the sections out of order. Doing so may not be my preference but I'm attempting to respect you, the reader.

I must not be selfish, naïve, or arrogant in regard to the manner in which you consume the content in this book. All I should be concerned with is that you consume it. When, how, where, and if that happens is your choice.

Novel, huh?

The Business Model

It's the space between the stories news outlets value currently.

The stories you produce are given away. The space in between them is sold to advertisers.

What if the contrary was true?

What if a market of interested parties assigned a monetary value to the content we produced rather than the spaces scattered in between that content, at least initially?

And what might happen if this valuation process were transparent? One in which the content creators, potential viewers, and interested advertisers all might have the opportunity to witness, impact, and benefit from.

In essence an exchange would be created.

A content exchange.

An exchange in which a market of interested parties valued content and in turn the space inside, around, and nearby that content.

Right now the dead space between stories has no intrinsic value. Its value is simply a derivative of the audience size created by the content we produce. The nature in which this value is determined is at best inaccurate and at worst fraudulent.

Television stations habitually skew viewership ratings. Sales associates spin, obfuscate, and categorize ratings in manners that often mask underperformance and exaggerate the product's influence on key demographics. Ad buyers are left with murky valuations and little choice other than to shift their business online.

In the meantime, television stations reduce costs, and subsequently quality, to cope with the shift in ad dollars.

Unless a set-top box, like Roku, emerges and is synchronized with each computer and mobile device in a household, accurate and transparently calculated values for advertising space are not realistic.

So what does that mean for content? If we cannot accurately value the advertising real estate scattered between our content how are we to value the content? An objective method is lacking in current business models.

Sure, subscription models exist. I'm certainly not disparaging subscription models. In fact, later I'll argue on behalf of subscriptions comprising a part of the next generation model. But that still does not answer the core question I posed earlier. What is our content worth if we cannot accurately measure our audiences or value the advertising space around it?

The answer is the exchange-like model I mentioned earlier.

We will add value for all involved only once we begin valuing individual pieces or packages of content. Only after we begin valuing content will we obtain the appropriate data to value the advertising opportunities that surround that content.

We must upend the current model which assigns value to advertising space rather than content. When we do this we will create greater value for our news outlets. We'll also arm ourselves with data that will allow us to make real time decisions regarding what we choose to cover, how we cover it, and the depth in which we cover it.

This in turn will create value for consumers of the content as well as those interested in creating advertisements within or around the content.

It's actually rather simple in theory.

Those in the market for content determine the value of that content as it is born, being created, and as it's distributed. Value is not static but rather fluid. Those in the market can, at any time, revalue a specific piece of content based upon the introduction or subtraction of other individual pieces of content.

Likewise, the value of the advertising potential within or around specific pieces of content will be derived, in part, from how the market values the content to which the advertising is attached.

The advertising is a derivative of the content.

Structuring the model in this manner removes much of the subjectivity, unfairness, and inaccuracy inherent in how television advertising space is valued currently.

The model I describe allows markets of interested parties to assign value. It provides a more objective means in regard to the setting of prices.

However, creating a content and advertising exchange will require television news outlets to do something currently considered sacrosanct. It requires television news outlets to give up the secrets they work to keep quiet all day long. It requires television news outlets to part with some of the perceived safety that comes from opacity.

It means you must reveal your rundown!

Expose it.

Show it to the world.

It'll feel as if you're naked.

You'll be showing your hand not only to potential viewers and advertisers but also to the competition. It's the present day equivalent of calling your competitors after the morning editorial meeting and telling them your plan of attack for the day.

This is the cardinal sin of television news, right?

No one wants their stories leaking to the competition.

Especially with ample time for competitors to duplicate the story and break it first.

Allowing the world to see your rundown early each morning violates everything we have been taught about creating a competitive newsroom. It relinquishes the competitive advantage we've been told we create by keeping it secret. Inviting the world to see our plan eliminates any hope we have of being proprietary for the day, right?

It's understandable if you feel this way.

But how is the status quo working out for you? Competing newscasts in any given market are nearly identical despite rundown opacity. Clinging to convention is not a strategy. Neither is hoping the decline in viewership ends. Nor is banking on the ad dollars that shifted online one day shifting back.

I wrote at the outset incremental change will not do.

By now I'm betting you're starting to understand that was a promise rather than a warning.

Your rundown, at least as you know it now, is the foundation for a thriving content and advertising exchange, or CAE.

The CAE is where you'll place potential content on the market. Your rundown, the CAE, is where the public will pass judgment on each and every piece. You'll still have the responsibility to set the agenda each morning. However, that agenda will undoubtedly be influenced as the market values each piece of potential content.

This is where it becomes a bit complicated.

By what means will the market value specific pieces of content?

One idea is to invite market participants to buy individual pieces or packages of content similar to the way investors and traders buy shares of publicly traded companies. We might build out the platform so market participants can buy and sell content prior to its completion and throughout the day as additional information is learned about the content and the pieces of competing content.

The value of a particular piece of content might rise and fall based on which pieces of content market participants most want to view.

For instance, if a new piece of content were introduced to the market several hours after the original pieces of content began trading, participants could buy the new piece if they're able. If not, they might be permitted to sell back the content they originally purchased so they can buy the new piece.

Should the new piece of content wind up not being as interesting or newsworthy as when it was originally introduced, market participants might rotate back into their original positions. Obviously, the introduction of new pieces of content throughout the day has the potential to impact the value of each piece that precedes them.

Simply put, the news outlet reveals what it believes is newsworthy early in the day. People then click on the pieces or packages of content they intend to buy and view upon completion. The data dictates which ideas actually become stories.

As the market determines the value of each piece of content so too is it determining how to price the advertising potential within and surrounding the content. Advertising, sponsorship, and placement opportunities will derive their values from how the market values the content to which the advertising is attached.

The advertising instruments associated with a piece of content, there can be several associated with each piece of content, will fluctuate in value based on their underlying content component. Advertisers will have opportunities to, in essence, bid for the rights to a specific advertising instrument.

Obviously, this model has major implications for how sales departments operate and are structured. Turn to page 108 if you'd like to learn how now.

Think of it as a stock exchange for news stories.

It's not necessarily the same as buying shares in a publicly traded company. But similar to a stock exchange, a news outlet might introduce story ideas in the morning and allow viewers to buy the pieces they want to view upon completion. The ideas most popular on the exchange are the ones we turn into stories.

As complex as building and operating a content exchange might sound, the platform we use to execute a CAE must be as simple and functional as possible. It will fail should anyone deem it too complicated or cumbersome in which to participate.

In reality, we're not asking people interested in a piece of content to purchase 100 shares and trade those shares throughout the day. We're asking them to pay for the content they want to view. And we're asking them to pay for it prior to the gathering, writing, and editing of the final product in some cases.

But we are not locking them in.

We are giving them an opportunity to change their minds once new information and new opportunities become available.

We're letting them see what we have on tap in the morning. We are inviting them to participate in the editorial process. They are voting with their money. They are purchasing the right to view only the content they want to see.

Should a new piece of content be placed on the exchange at some point in the day each market participant will be notified. They will then have the opportunity to add to their content cart and purchase the new piece of content if they choose. Those with the financial means can add content throughout the day. Those with more meager financial means will have the choice to sell the content they purchased earlier in the day should they be more interested in a newer piece of content.

Financial markets do not provide do-overs.

The CAE does.

That's why it's beautiful. And that's how it'll build trust lacking in financial markets.

The transparency this model provides is evident. It allows people to choose the content they want to see. It allows them to change their minds. But it also ensures that content creators are paid.

Premium options may be added to provide people with an even greater degree of choice.

For instance, market participants might choose to pay an additional sum to receive the content prior to others who have paid a lesser sum of money. Or a group of market participants might choose to pay an additional sum to receive the content without any type of advertising, sponsorship, or placement. Participants might also want the option to share the content, save it to a personal clipboard, or talk directly to the creator of the content.

None of these options is guaranteed to succeed or fail.

That's the beauty of the model. It enables decision makers to routinely introduce new options and choices. It allows for continual experimentation and inventiveness. The model is inherently social which means you'll get real time feedback.

Market research will take on a whole new meaning for those who adopt all or part of the model.

The model also makes the process more transparent and valuable for entities wishing to bid on the advertising instruments attached to the content. Advertisers will be able to see in real time what viewers value most in terms of content. They'll know for certain which piece of content is most valuable to the viewers they'd like to influence.

The model empowers advertisers and enables them to narrow their advertising strategy based on their budgets and objectives. Rather than reserving a spot in the late news as they do currently, this model allows advertisers to bid on the exact spot they want. The one they believe will generate the greatest return. Here again, premium options may be added to provide advertisers with an even greater degree of choice.

For instance, advertisers who are not the high bidder for a particular instrument may be offered lump sum payment options for various placement opportunities. Or an entity might choose to pay a lump sum to guarantee they are not outbid for a certain instrument in the open market. They might also be willing to pay for shared stakes in a variety of instruments linked to multiple pieces of content.

As with consumers, advertisers would be able to sell sponsorships should they become more valuable later or if they suddenly become more interested in an instrument underlying a new piece of content. For instance, an advertiser whose instrument dramatically increases in value may sell the instrument for a profit to another advertiser. The model provides opportunity and flexibility where once little or none existed.

It's not hard to see entrepreneurs seizing on the opportunity, starting businesses, and buying up advertising instruments they believe will increase in value.

Additionally, the transparency of the model also serves to benefit the news outlets managing it. The CAE puts your content and the right to advertise in or around it up for auction each day. The higher the quality of content you produce the more money you are able to earn from two different streams.

Those who are creative can add to or adapt the model to develop additional revenue streams.

For instance, the exchange offers news outlets a plethora of data about the entities wanting to advertise in or around your content. Very soon observant news outlets will notice patterns in the data. They will use that data to better market advertising opportunities that exist outside the exchange.

Advertisers will, by default, create a composite sketch of their advertising tastes based upon their bidding histories. Entities outside the news business will likely find these sketches valuable as well. A database may be created based on this history and used as a proprietary stream of revenue separate from the news product itself.

Likewise, news outlets will also collect data from market participants who consume the content produced. The content these exchange participants bid on will create a clearer picture of who the people are as customers. More specifically, the types of content participants purchase provide outlets with qualitative data that often proves so elusive to retailers and other marketers who routinely monitor social media for hints and clues.

Here again, those adopting this model can create for themselves an additional stream of revenue.

Besides purchase histories, consumers will also provide news outlets with information about specific advertisements. More specifically, for how long did they watch the advertisement? At what point did they stop watching? What part of the advertisement was a hit and what part did not work?

Some of this data can be teased out socially and in real time. The data will no doubt be of value to advertisers participating in the exchange and non-participants outside the exchange.

Another benefit of the exchange is the advantage it provides managers in terms of how they select content. The exchange model allows news managers to make data driven decisions based on what's trending. No longer must news managers sit in editorial meetings and wonder what people might want or need to consume.

When they notice market participants are flocking to a specific story they'll be able to make real time decisions to capitalize on the trend.

For instance, if people are gravitating toward a particular story, a news manager might decide to assign additional resources to the topic. Doing so might allow a bounce piece to be created in the shadow of the original story. People choosing to pay to see one might be more apt to pay to see the bounce piece as well.

Likewise, an advertiser's interest may be leveraged in this manner. The top bidder on the original trending story might be contacted ahead of the bounce piece being placed on the market. Or the original high bid advertiser may be offered a special deal to sponsor both pieces. Additionally, an even bigger package may be sold to the advertiser should the prospect of follow up coverage the next day be mentioned as a possibility.

Here again, value is created for each of the parties involved.

Creating unique and ongoing advertising opportunities for clearly popular content allows advertisers the ability to better connect with viewers. For instance, an advertiser who agrees to purchase instruments derived from the original trending piece, the bounce piece, and the follow up piece tomorrow dramatically expands the likelihood of connecting with those they wish to influence.

Rather than creating a single advertisement for a single piece the entity that purchased all three instruments can structure an advertisement accordingly. The advertiser may be able to create an ongoing story that is more likely to touch its intended audience. In essence, the package allows the advertiser to engage in a type of ongoing storytelling it would not be afforded in a single instance.

Conversely, bounce piece instruments may also be offered to competitors of the entity bidding on the instrument linked to the original trending content.

The model also allows you to structure the exchange in a manner that allows the crowd to dictate whether its content contains advertisements at all. More specifically, a news manager might set a certain financial threshold for a particular piece of content. If market participants meet that threshold they'll receive the content without advertisements, sponsorships, or placements.

This serves a dual purpose.

Not only does it empower the crowd and allow it to determine what role, if any, an advertiser plays but it also serves to limit the amount of advertising space available to entities interested in bidding on the instruments linked to content. The practice increases the scarcity of advertising opportunities in a given marketplace.

Increase the scarcity of your advertising instruments and you'll likely increase demand.

It means the advertising instruments remaining will increase in value.

An advertiser might even be given the opportunity to meet the financial threshold, similar to a sponsorship, on behalf of viewers. Or an advertiser might swoop in after consumers have reached a financial threshold, match the dollar amount, and allow consumers to receive refunds thanks to the generosity of the sponsor.

It also enables news organizations to better diversify their revenue streams.

Additionally, the instruments attached to less popular content may be packaged and offered to advertising entities that have been priced out of trending or more highly valued content.

We've yet to touch on the human element of the exchange. More specifically, the exchange will finally allow news outlets to leverage and exploit the notoriety of their more popular talent.

Adding the name of an influential reporter to a piece of content may dramatically influence the value the market places on the piece. It should also inspire news outlets to promote individual pieces of content in ways they never have.

Like the sales department, adopting a model similar to this one has immense strategic and operational implications for a promotions department.

If attaching a specific reporter to a piece of content routinely adds a premium to the value of the content, an opportunity exists. A news outlet may leverage that opportunity by selling advertising packages, sponsorships, or brand placement opportunities based on the reporter with which the entity would like to be associated.

Additional opportunities exist when you consider the various ways you might use reporter notoriety to target viewers who have in the past shown a preference for that reporter.

For instance, if your database were to alert you that a particular viewer has been absent from the exchange for a period of time you might contact that person with a special offer based upon their past purchase habits. More specifically, should you identify the targeted person disproportionately purchases stories from a specific reporter you might offer a targeted package deal containing the last six stories the particular reporter has completed and the viewer has missed.

Before sending the offer smart news managers will of course cross the particular viewer's advertisement engagement preferences. They'll also determine which advertisers have sponsored the reporter in the past.

The strategy uses data generated on the exchange to create new streams of revenue outside the exchange. It identifies users who have not participated in the exchange in some time. It identifies advertising opportunities because of the participant's absence. Ultimately, the data matches the preferences of both parties so that value is created for each.

The absentee is provided a deal on content created by her favorite reporter. The advertiser is provided an opportunity to market with permission and in a manner that respects the prospect. And the news outlet generates revenue from linking the two.

The elasticity of the model is what makes it so effective.

It may be pulled, pushed, or stretched any way a news outlet needs for it to be successful. Of course, the absentee example is just one in which the model enables smart managers to earn money and goodwill thanks to data and the ingenuity to marry disparate pieces.

For instance, a news outlet may create opportunities off the exchange based on the prior day's exchange attendance. Anyone signed up who did not participate in the exchange may be contacted the following day with a special offer. You might compile the top five or ten trendiest stories from the day prior. You might strategically match the special offer with specific advertising partnerships.

You might offer an exchange participant a piece of content for free, or first, simply because they participate often. A variety of ways exist in terms of rewarding loyalty and to connect with your viewers.

Similar opportunities exist in terms of cultivating advertising relationships. You might attach the advertising entity's brand or key message to a piece of content being sent to exchange participants for free.

News outlets are only limited in how they use and build upon the exchange by their creativity.

If you're bothered by how labor intensive the exchange sounds in regard to consumer participation you can easily transform the exchange into a subscription service. For instance, people can subscribe to the exchange for a flat monthly fee and select the stories you're creating to view later in the day. You're still collecting the data you need to better match advertisers with consumers.

However, this removes a bit of the social nature in the exchange as I originally described it. A subscription model may end up winning out though. In that respect you might want to treat a subscription similar to the way wireless companies treat data plans.

For consumers on a finite content plan, news outlets would be required to notify consumers when their usage is nearing the limit of their plan. You might charge overage fees should someone consume more content then than their plan allows in a given month.

You might also offer an unlimited consumption plan to consumers who routinely run over their content usage limits. You might also consider innovative ways to treat people who do not use all of their allotted consumption for the month.

Unused content may be converted into content credits.

Might you allow content credits to roll over to the next month similar to rollover wireless minutes? These content credits are valuable and you must realize that.

Might you also create an additional section on the exchange where people might trade or sell their unused content credits? The exchange operator would collect a transaction fee while also giving participants with unused content credits a way to monetize them. Such a model would also allow participants about to exceed their usage limits a way to purchase additional content credits at a discount to the overage fees charged by the exchange operator.

The model assumes news outlets will, at some point, begin charging money for their content. Only those creating premium content will be able to successfully charge a premium for their content. For readers looking for ideas in regard to creating premium content, please see *A Model Reporter Model* on page 148.

However, I'm certain there are some of you who do not subscribe to the notion viewers will ultimately pay for digital news content. If that's the case, the model is adaptable to your hypothesis.

Rather than asking exchange participants to trade capital for content, news managers can adapt the model so participants are trading social capital for content. The potential exists for content to be valued based upon its social popularity.

Adapting the model in this manner allows you to use likes, comments, and retweets etc. in place of currency. You might even consider creating your own form of social currency for use in the market. The market will still be assigning a value to the content it views it just won't be a value denominated in dollars and cents.

It means you'll also forgo a revenue stream.

While I'm not optimistic news outlets will remain viable without some form of premium or paid content as part of their business model, the idea does allow us to explore another potential revenue stream: influence.

Big money may be made from measuring influence.

Content valued by social capital presents an opportunity to identify, catalogue, and leverage social influence. Similar to Klout scores, keeping tabs on social influence may allow news organizations to construct influence scores.

Influence scores may one day impact whether we qualify for a credit card, are offered a job, or what kind of interest rate we are offered on a mortgage. Retailers and marketers are chomping at the bit to identify people with the most influence. The theory is if you can influence the influencers you'll no doubt sell more product.

However, social scientists have questioned the impact of influence. Some argue like-minded people tend to migrate toward and congregate with one another. They argue these people are really not influencing one another but rather reinforcing purchase decisions each would have made individually.

The debate is outside the scope of this book.

I simply highlight it here so you are aware of the potential pitfalls in attempting to monetize influence.

That said, calculating influence scores based on data gleaned from the exchange may be one way to generate revenue while continuing to offer your content for free. I'm not advocating it. I'm simply providing an alternative for those who do not believe exchange participants will be willing to pay for content.

A hybrid model may also be created. For instance, a participant may not have to pay until after they consume a certain number of stories. Or participants may get three free pieces for each piece they purchase. The possibilities are exciting and virtually endless.

No matter what you believe about charging money for your content, the exchange model outlined here is a much more transparent, accurate, and efficient way to value the content we create.

And the advertising space in and around it.

Not only does it enable us to better connect content consumers with advertisers but it also provides news outlets a variety of revenue streams. More importantly, an exchange-based model allows news outlets to create value for each of the exchange's participants.

That's much more than we can say for the current model.

Promoting the Exchange

A news outlet's promotions department will be forced to reinvent itself should the exchange model be adopted.

The exchange is highly social and so too must a promotions department that wants to squeeze every bit of value from it. The biggest obstacle a promotions department must overcome is its mindset. More specifically, promotions departments are in the business of teasing audiences. Building intrigue and giving away only enough to entice outsiders to tune in.

Present day promotions efforts are long in the tooth. They're asking people to view content that may not actually be broadcast for hours. They're asking people to set aside whatever they had planned on doing to consume the piece being teased.

Topicals are no better. Most are ineffective, vague, and do not create any value for the viewer. Additionally, most tease writers should not be writing teases. Many lack an understanding of the nuances inherent in writing news.

That's why it is often the tease that lands a station in legal hot water.

It's time for promotions departments, at least in their current form, to go.

Teases are for strippers.

They're for pole dancers.

They're for girls who dance for g-string cash.

Not for news outlets attempting to regain relevance and build reputations based on creating value for those who consume their content.

Not that news outlets adopting the exchange model have much of a choice but to overhaul the manner in which their promotions departments operate. Traditional teases aim to benefit the tease creator rather than the viewer. This is not consistent with our overarching goal of creating value for viewers.

Unlike stock in publicly traded companies, an exchange created by a news outlet does not come equipped with universal opening and closing bells. Each piece of content created is unique. So too is its shelf life.

Unlike shares in public companies, pieces of content do not uniformly start and stop trading hands at a predetermined time. That's what makes content unique. Content is created.

It may be modified. It may be added to or subtracted from. Each is an opportunity for the news outlet running the exchange to create value.

And each is an opportunity for promotions to help the outlet extract additional value. A next generation promotions department will be tasked with increasing margins. When a promotions operative notices something trending he or she will work quickly to leverage the popularity.

Likewise, and maybe more importantly, promotions operatives must proactively seek out less popular content and identify why it lacks popularity. If it's not trending or gaining financial support because it is not premium in nature it is futile for promotions to attempt triage. Remember, teases are for strippers not news content. We must make the transition from marketers back to news breakers.

However, should the operative learn the issue is one of messaging, placement, or packaging he or she can quickly alter that dynamic and improve the content's chances of gaining financial popularity.

The lack of time and space constraints are what make the exchange model so exciting. We are no longer limited by either space or time in terms of creating premium content. The more premium content we create the more value we create for everyone.

News outlets will only be limited by the size of the addressable market to which they are appealing. More specifically, exchange participants in pursuit of premium content have only a finite amount of money to spend on content. Similarly, advertisers may bid on the instruments attached to the content only as far as their marketing budgets will allow.

However, until you max out your addressable market your goal should be the continued creation of premium content. Your secondary goal must be to promote that content in a manner that generates the greatest rate of return.

Again, smart promotions will ensure news outlets maximize their margins.

But how do we create smart promotions?

Remember, we're not going to tease exchange participants in the traditional sense. But we must equip them with the information they'll need to make good choices in terms of the content they select for purchase.

This will allow for a dual benefit.

Not only will news outlets be providing exchange participants with information regarding the shelf life of the content in which they are interested, they will also be creating a sense of urgency that will benefit the outlet itself.

Exchange participants must know how long they have to purchase content. While opportunities will exist later to purchase packages of content, those purchasing individual pieces of content on the exchange must always be given progress updates in regard to the content in which they are interested.

We can accomplish this in a variety of ways.

Each is analogous to an idea created and executed by Dominos Pizza (DPZ). Dominos sells approximately one-third of its pizzas online (data current as of 5/2013). One reason for Dominos' success is the social nature of the ordering process.

A large component of that process includes Dominos' pizza tracker feature.

Just because you've ordered doesn't mean Dominos is finished communicating with you. The contrary is true. The pizza tracker is a way Dominos provides value to carryout customers after the sale.

The pizza tracker shows customers where their pizza is at in the cooking process. It's a step by step update. It tells customers how long they have before their pizza is finished cooking. It enables them to time their trip to the store. It empowers customers and reduces the odds a pizza will lose its fresh-from-the-oven taste before a customer can pick up the pizza.

It ensures customers get a piping hot pizza and creates value after the sale.

Dominos doesn't have to do it.

But it does so because it realizes the benefits of making transactions more social.

A similar strategy may be employed by next generation news outlets.

I use Dominos as an example rather than a rule. You might choose to structure your story tracker differently. You might choose to create something similar to the tool we see that updates us in regard to file downloads. Maybe you'll choose to send text alerts to those who have purchased the story. Or update those who have purchased similar stories in the past. Or you might tweet the status of the story.

You might also consider promoting how an individual's behavior compares with other exchange participants. An individual's purchase decision may be reinforced should it be one a majority of others have also selected for consumption. Conversely, an individual might be congratulated for their unique taste when their selection is not popular among other participants.

How you execute a promotional strategy is less important than ensuring you emphasize the urgency inherent in the exchange.

Content consumers interested in purchasing premium services from your news outlet must be made aware of the time decay involved in the creation of the content.

Promotions departments might still send movie-like trailers to smartphones. They may also promote the urgency outside the exchange. They may also use a quick video status update from the reporter currently creating the story to sell the piece to exchange participants who have a history of purchasing stories created by that reporter.

Promotions will also be responsible for creating urgency among advertisers, notifying them when a piece of content is trending, or how long they have left to bid on a highly sought after advertising derivative.

Each of these targeted promotions is an opportunity to sell sponsorships. For instance, each time a reporter attaches a 12-second update on the content he is creating on the exchange, the news outlet is provided an opportunity to sell.

These opportunities may be auctioned off or included in packaged deals or both. Again, remember news outlets using this model will no longer be constrained by time and space.

It means as long as you are producing premium content you are affording yourself endless opportunities to sell advertisements, sponsorships, or placements.

I can't emphasize enough the limitless possibilities for news managers who adopt an exchange-like model.

Again, you're only limited by your imagination.

The data you generate via the exchange will provide targeted promotional opportunities that do not exist today.

Remember, I mentioned promotions operatives must adopt a new mindset if they are to navigate, leverage, and succeed with an exchange-like model. This means they, similar to the content producers, must eliminate what I call the "mass mindset".

We're not broadcasting to the masses via the exchange. Rather we are creating content for specific groups of people willing to financially support and commit to viewing such content. We know ahead of time the content is desirable. We don't wait for the ratings to be released to see if people viewed or preferred our content to someone else's. With the exchange we know ahead of time. We know prior to making a mistake. We acquire real time data about select viewer groups and can adjust accordingly.

The same must happen in terms of promotional execution.

We are no longer promoting to the masses. Targeted personal promotions that deliver value or prevent a consumer from missing something he or she might enjoy are now the jobs of promotions operatives.

Think of yourself as the Amazon of news content. Not only will you have a participant's purchase history but you'll also have data illustrating their exchange browsing history. You'll have data outlining their social connections and what they're friends are browsing and buying. This puts you in a position to make personal recommendations just like Amazon does.

It allows exchange participants to create wish lists. It allows their friends and families to fulfill those wishes.

Not only does the technology exist but it is also being used in different applications.

Scientists at the Technical University of Madrid have created software that recommends web content based on a consumer's past usage. It has been tested on 70,000 users who report the model is highly accurate in recommending content they'd like to see.

Researchers are now attempting to determine whether the software has any commercial potential.

Using this type of technology will enable news managers to understand an exchange participant's preferences and recommend content based on those preferences. You'll also recommend content based upon the preferences of their social networks. Marketing and promoting your content in this manner will be less obtrusive. It'll communicate that you know your consumer on a level not possible in a bygone era.

The data will be at our fingertips. So let's use it. Consumer content profiles will exist and dictate how we seek permission to market to specific individuals. One size no longer fits all. Promotions operatives will reap rewards one consumer at a time. Initially, promotions operatives will see their goal as getting a consumer to purchase a piece of content.

That is the wrong mindset.

It is selfishly transparent and disrespectful to those participating in the CAE. The mindset that must be adopted by promotions operatives is one of value creation. If we create value for the consumer they will in turn create value for our news outlet.

This has major implications on who news outlets choose to hire. Promotions teams may be better off stacked with entrepreneurial-minded business degree holders than traditional marketers.

The mindset is the key to unlocking value from the exchange.

The Pitch Store

Next generation news outlets will certainly not have a monopoly on premium content ideas.

The key is to expand the pool of ideas and create additional revenue streams along the way. Right now, news outlets are leaving money on the table in terms of the ideas that are voluntarily sent their way. Newsrooms are repositories for ideas.

Ideas have value.

Unfortunately though, we toss the majority of those ideas in the garbage.

More specifically, I'm referring to news releases, media alerts, and story pitches. The majority of these never make a newscast. We discard most without reading them thoroughly. We routinely delete news releases that do not include a newsworthy email subject line.

Why?

A variety of reasons exist including the fact many PR staffers do not understand what makes something newsworthy or how to properly frame a pitch. However, news reporters are at fault as well for not making the time to find the diamond in the mess. Ultimately, there's enough blame to go around. I'm not concerned with whose fault it is and neither should you.

I'm concerned with extracting the value inherent in many of these pitches.

Rather than dumping them in the trash, deleting them, or ignoring them altogether why don't we build a platform that creates value for the PR staffers pitching us? Should we do so we'll be giving exchange participants more choice in terms of potential content. We'll also create an additional revenue stream for our news outlet.

It's a win, win, win situation.

Here's how it might work. Just as there is allegedly a line between the sales and news departments in present day television stations, only crossed when a story may jeopardize ad dollars, we must create some sort of barrier between the original content we are creating in our newsrooms and the content being pushed by PR outfits.

The solution is *The Pitch Store*.

The Pitch Store is a separate section of the exchange where PR outfits can submit news releases. News outlets may choose to charge PR outfits a fee for each submission, offer a subscription to *The Pitch Store*, or monetize the opportunity via sponsorship or in some other way. Clearly though, this is an opportunity for PR staffers to get their news releases in front of people actively seeking newsworthy content.

News releases must no longer die in a reporter's email in-box.

Exchange participants are not generally perusing wires where news releases are dumped. *The Pitch Store* affords PR outfits a more narrow and engaging opportunity than a wire service might.

Should a particular pitch draw enough interest from exchange participants it may be selected for inclusion on the exchange. The news outlet may incorporate the pitch into the content it creates that day.

Revenue generated from exchange participants purchasing content inclusive of the PR pitch would be shared in some manner with the PR outfit that originally pitched the idea. So too would revenue received from advertisers bidding on the instruments connected to the content. Thus, PR outfits including their pitches in *The Pitch Store* would have the opportunity to make money on the exchange. You're creating a financial incentive for PR firms to improve their ideas and pitches.

The value created is bountiful.

You're empowering consumers with additional choices and the ability to select content the news outlet originally might have missed, ignored, or not selected.

You're also creating a previously untapped revenue stream: PR firms floating news releases on behalf of clients.

And you're also generating additional revenue for your news outlet and exposing yourself to content with the ability to increase the quality of the content you produce.

That's not all though.

Here again creativity and inventiveness will rule the day on the exchange you build. For instance, a PR firm might notice a release it provided *The Pitch Store* logically supplements an unrelated piece of content the news outlet is promoting on the exchange. Regardless of whether the pitch becomes popular in *The Pitch Store*, a news outlet might creatively offer PR firms with legitimate content an opportunity to sponsor the piece of content currently being created on the exchange.

This would expose the pitch in some manner to people who otherwise might not have been exposed to the PR firm's pitch. Remember, you must allow the data you've gathered to dictate when these sponsorships are likely to provide value. Should the sponsorship be perceived as intrusive you risk losing an exchange participant.

Sponsorship pricing will be contingent upon how the market values the content, the shelf life of the content, and how the advertising instruments attached to the content are being valued. Crossover from *The Pitch Store* to the exchange will only be successful if it is done judiciously. Crossover must be handled with precision, care, and personalization. Sponsorships from *The Pitch Store* must be narrowly targeted if they are to be successful in creating value for each party involved. If not, sponsorships are likely to backfire and cause your outlet reputational harm.

The Pitch Store also provides news outlets an opportunity to create additional value for entities interested in advertising with the outlet. Once exchange participants begin engaging with content from *The Pitch Store* advertisers may become attracted to the idea of a more subtle way of influencing.

Rather than overtly advertising, an entity interested in subtle advertising may wish to create content for display in *The Pitch Store*. News outlets will obviously be available to help with this.

It's similar to present day creative services departments that help advertisers create commercials for broadcast. Next generation news outlets will have professional news writers available to construct news releases, media alerts, or social pitches for advertisers who wish to influence consumers via *The Pitch Store*.

Or news organizations might connect those in search of these services with PR firms or marketers already using *The Pitch Store*.

Besides creating another avenue in which advertisers may influence consumers and possibly earn money by being chosen for inclusion in the exchange, news outlets are also working on behalf of consumers who might prefer a less obtrusive form of advertising.

Once again, the news outlet creates another stream of revenue by offering this service. Outlets will likely experiment with various pricing models before finding one most beneficial to each party involved. However, it should be clear by now how value is determined on the exchange.

The Pitch Store will become a searchable idea repository that extracts value from ideas that were tossed in the garbage during a bygone era. It's a safe bet that *The Pitch Store* will elevate the quality of news releases, media alerts, and social pitches.

Currently, the majority are tossed because they lack newsworthiness, a counterintuitive angle, or are poorly written and overly promotional. However, once PR firms are confronted with an opportunity to transform their news releases into money makers, it's a safe bet they'll dramatically increase the quality of their pitches.

Ultimately, they'll serve their clients better.

They'll make money when they are successful in their pitches.

Exchange participants will enjoy content they might not have in the past.

And everyone will have you, the next generation news outlet, to thank.

The Vault

Your vault is gathering dust.

It's not earning a dime.

In fact it's costing you to maintain, convert, and preserve.

Why on earth is your archive an expense rather than a revenue generator?

In case you've been asleep for the last several sections and are just waking up now, the next generation news product business model is narrowly focused on extracting and creating value. But before I show you several ways you might do this with your archive system, let's briefly acquaint ourselves with the current reality.

News stations produce content, offer it to the public in a limited fashion, and then post it to the web as an afterthought. After the content is broadcast it is pushed offstage and relegated to the web.

After spending a few hours on the front of your website it is pushed to the back to make room for newer content.

In essence, we produce content and then hide it almost immediately.

This makes no sense and is telling in terms of how news stations themselves value what they produce. Why are news stations so quick to hide their content?

If you're going to argue it's because you are continually providing viewers with so much new and engaging content I would ask you to find a mirror and take an honest look at yourself and your station's ratings.

The content you create shouldn't die shortly after it's created. But television news stations seem intent on murdering it. Afterward, they bury it so it's never heard from or seen again.

Are we covering our tracks because we know we've committed a crime?

Rather than viewing our archives as an expense useful only for pulling file video from time to time, we'd be smart to unlock the value inside. Archive maintenance and preservation ought not to be a chore. Rather our archives must be marketed and perceived as repositories of history. Vaults where we lock and store valuables deserving of protection.

We should no longer hide our archives from the world. In fact, archives can be extremely valuable for those apt to use them creatively.

Just ask Google.

The company generated $14 billion in revenue in its first fiscal quarter of 2013. Google archives the world's data and enables people to instantaneously find specific pieces. News outlets, with their vast amounts of content, would be smart to become smaller local versions of Google.

Right now you're working for your archive.

It's time to make your archive work for you.

More specifically, an exchange-like model positions news outlets to offer additional content based on current purchasing trends as well as exchange participant profiles. Creating a smart archive allows you to provide add-on services and content to a variety of participants.

A variety of ways exist to monetize your archive.

Obviously care must be taken to ensure premium content is not made available for free to the masses shortly after exchange participants pay for it. Aside from that precaution, news outlets must make their archives easily searchable.

Ease of use is key here.

Many television news archives are archaic and not user-friendly. The archive you allow the public to use must be easy to use, just like Google. Google is the standard by which you'll be compared. So be prepared to invest in making your archive easy to search and quick to produce results.

Whether to charge for the content in your archive is likely a more difficult decision. However, it is a question that may have a hybrid-like answer. The content you offer for free via your news outlet should ultimately remain free in your archive.

Conversely, the content purchased in some manner on your exchange may better serve its creator by remaining for purchase in the archive. Obviously, premium content may be discounted based on its age or relevance.

To be consistent though, it's probably best to allow archive users to determine the value of the premium content in your archive. The content that is searched for the most will obviously be more valuable than content that is rarely searched for.

The argument to be had here is one in which both sides can make strong arguments.

Premium content behind a paywall and purchased initially must be protected, some would argue. The integrity of the content is contingent upon maintaining some sort of pricing power in regard to the content. If you train people to wait until content is free you destroy the ability to charge on the exchange.

However, there's also an argument to be made to pattern one's archive after Google. Enable people to search for and find content of interest and deliver it to them free of charge. You might sell display advertisements around the searches. Either way, your archive strategy should be constructed in a way that creates additional revenue streams.

Or you might create an entire new way to monetize your archive. In cases where the premium content you've created will undoubtedly be searched for and viewed for sometime, you might offer advertisers a chance to sponsor the content for life. Under this scenario, advertisers would buy the right to sponsor the content for the duration of the content's life. Doing so might preclude the news outlet from charging people who are searching for it. It would, in essence, be a gift from the advertiser to those seeking the content.

You might also create several additional levels to the advertising instruments on which entities bid via the exchange. An additional sum of money might guarantee the content remains attached to an advertisement for a predetermined amount of time. An even larger sum may guarantee attachment for the life of the content.

You might also use your archive to supplement the content consumers purchase on the exchange. For instance, trending content with a long history to your consumers creates an opportunity for you to over deliver. Once the content is completed and ready for consumption you might make available for free the last three stories you have done on the topic. This provides exchange participants with added value. It also provides news outlets with another way to monetize their archives.

These archived packages to be offered for free may be offered as opportunities for advertisers to reach and influence consumers in a more cost-effective way than say bidding on advertising instruments via the exchange.

Additionally, corporations, public safety departments, and lawyers, anyone who appears in your news product frequently, may be interested in purchasing clips of past appearances. Besides posterity, these clips or "best of" compilations may be marketed in a manner that creates demand where once there was none. More specifically, news outlets that routinely cover high school sports will quickly want to unlock the value hidden in their archives. High school athletes mentioned during newscasts may be marketed as keepsakes and gifts.

You might even auction popular search terms should your archive become popular enough.

Creativity and experimentation will ultimately yield a specific monetization strategy.

Here again, you're only limited by your creativity.

However, your archive, based in the cloud, is not the only archive you'll oversee.

News outlets would be smart to create archives for each of their exchange participants. Each participant should have their own cloud-based vault where they can store the content they've purchased, clipped, or traded with social contacts.

Providing individual vaults increases the social engagement of those participating in your exchange.

I'm certain you're wondering about purchased content and how that might be shared. Video content, by nature, is to be shared, traded, and spread among social contacts today. But I often hear the argument that charging money for video content eliminates the social nature of video sharing. I hear critics argue you remove the ability to share video and the potential for it to go viral when you charge money for it.

I disagree.

Paid video content may still be traded and shared among social contacts. I'm certainly not advocating we prevent people from selecting a piece of premium content in their vault and sending it to friends.

The contrary is true.

We want exchange participants to share the videos they've purchased. We just don't want those they've shared with to have the ability to fully consume the video until they've paid a price. More specifically, video content that is shared with social contacts should be viewable to a degree. Contacts might be able to watch the first 15 seconds. Or innovative stations might embed code in the file that recognizes the file has been shared and automatically shows the recipient a movie-like trailer or synopsis of the video for purchase.

We must also be mindful to create incentives for sharing purchased content. For instance, news outlets may offer recipients of shared content a discount to purchase. Or recipients may be offered some other type of promotion that allows them to sample the content for free in exchange for a longer term financial commitment to the exchange.

Additional opportunities exist not only to monetize your cloud-based archive and those of your participants, but also to attract new users to your product.

More specifically, an opportunity exists to sell archive subscriptions to school districts and universities. While financially advantageous, the revenue stream created here is not what's important.

Exposing your product to elementary-aged students is extremely important in terms of building an audience. These are digital natives who will have likely grown up without being routinely exposed to a traditional newscast. Your history, accomplishments, and place in the community are completely foreign to this group.

Your archive can fill that gap.

Not only will a moderately priced archive subscription serve as an educational tool teachers can use in the classroom, but it will also serve as a product sample for students in those classrooms. Students will grow accustomed to turning to your news outlet despite having grown up without routinely sampling traditional newscasts. Offering your archive for educational or research purposes is not only a public service but also a recruiting tool stamped with the authority of the teacher using it.

Monetizing news archives is long overdue.

News outlets have been leaving money on the table for decades.

It's high time they started collecting what's theirs.

Connection Selling

Reinventing how television news sells itself to the world is an obvious requirement at this point. The strategies and tactics your sales team have used for decades instantly become irrelevant once you adopt a variation of the exchange model. Your sales operations simply were not designed to meet the demands of an exchange-based model.

Managing exchange sales differs substantially from the television station status quo in three ways:

- Selling vs. Connecting
- Real time capability
- Multiple stream management

Once your outlet has adopted an exchange model you'll no longer be selling in the traditional sense. Remember, the exchange upends conventional wisdom which currently has you selling the dead space between content blocks.

Presently, selling television news advertisements is impersonal, opaque, and fraudulent when viewer ratings are manipulated or skewed. The reality is present day sales techniques have little or no chance of succeeding on an exchange-based model.

In fact, you must adopt a different mindset if you are to successfully attract advertising revenue to the exchange.

You'll have to stop selling and start connecting.

Once an exchange-based model is adopted a traditional sales department must understand it is now in the business of making connections. Connections are the lifeblood of an exchange. The more connections you make the more revenue you generate. It's a transactional process that, if nurtured correctly, continually creates value for each party and never actually ends.

Who are you connecting?

A better question might be who and what you aren't connecting? Your role now is to connect people with ideas, advertisers to targeted audiences, and content with entities that deem it valuable. Data generated from the exchange will guide who you connect and when you connect them.

Connections are to be targeted, specific, and valuable to each party.

It's far different from the current model where a sales associate might spend a substantial amount of time closing a large deal with an advertiser who purchases a large block of broadcast air time.

Rather the next generation model demands routinely creating highly personalized connections. And it demands you do so quickly and in real time. These connections are created continuously and often without additional future commitments. You'll no longer be able to blankly sell into the future since you won't know what type of content is in demand or being created in the future.

Herein lies the exchange's second substantial difference with the current model: real time capability.

Advertising instruments will often be sold in real time. The exchange creates an auction-like framework your sales staff will have to navigate to make connections that count. And those are the only kind that generate value for the parties involved.

It's your job to monitor how pieces of content on the exchange are being valued and by whom. Likewise, it's important you monitor which advertisers are bidding on instruments linked to specific content. It will also be your responsibility to gauge interest from participants in *The Pitch Store*.

Data from each of these areas will allow you to make better connections.

An advertiser that may be bidding on a specific instrument may be informed the exchange participants bidding on the linked content are not necessarily members of a key audience the advertiser is interested in attempting to influence. A news outlet may then recommend a piece of content that would connect the advertiser to a more desirable audience.

A sales team is simultaneously recommending content to exchange participants, informing them of content their social connections are consuming, and introducing them to related material from the vault they might have missed and might improve their comprehension of the content in which they are currently interested.

This example alone provides a plethora of opportunities for connection making.

The alert regarding the content social connections are consuming is an opportunity to connect an advertiser with a target audience it wishes to influence. Sponsorship opportunities also exist when related content is offered from the vault. Likewise, a sales team may then expose connected parties to the potential for further engagement.

Remember, you are matching consumers with advertisers in a manner that creates value for both. You are no longer marketing to the masses, at least in the traditional sense. Your role is to ensure consumers and advertisers find one another amid all of the consumption opportunities that exist online.

The user profiles, engagement histories, and real time valuations are the data that will empower you to create value by bringing together disparate parties. The individual pieces you'll have in front of you- content, exchange participants, advertisers, archive browsers, *Pitch Store* participants- are pieces of a puzzle. A sales staff is the conduit that enables the pieces to fit together in the most efficient and valuable manner.

It's these different pieces that illustrate the third main difference between the status quo and the connection selling model of the future: multiple stream management.

Clearly, the next generation exchange-based news model, in whatever form it takes, creates revenue streams not envisioned or currently possible. However, it's important to understand the meandering nature of these streams. The revenue streams created under an exchange-based model are anything but stiff, rigid, or uncompromising.

In fact, they routinely mingle, cross, and intersect in ways limited only by a sales team's creativity, inventiveness, and desire to innovate. More specifically, these new revenue streams should not be viewed in vacuums. In fact, separate revenue streams that mingle create the potential for accelerated revenue growth.

It's not cross-selling like big banks attempt to execute.

It simply means that each stream derives a bit of its value from another stream. Once a stream derives enough value to consistently generate revenue, that stream may then be leveraged to create value or participate in another stream's growth.

I've already outlined several of the revenue streams an exchange-based model provides for. However, additional opportunities exist for those interested in leveraging the proprietary data they've collected. Below are several additional ways to use the data collected from the exchange to create tertiary streams of revenue.

Advertising Solutions

You'll intimately understand the advertising consumption habits of exchange participants. You'll understand which advertisements audiences have sampled, which they paid no mind to, and which were partially consumed. Technology also exists so that you might determine where in an advertisement a consumer stopped consuming. Finding out why is of even greater importance. To gather this data you might offer an exchange participant free content, access to a premium section of your outlet, or connect them with a special offer from an advertiser they routinely engage with. The data you collect about which advertisements were consumed, why, and exactly where and why a consumer stopped consuming an advertisement are invaluable to those constructing advertisements. How involved you'd like to become is up to you and the advertiser interested in the data you've collected. You might simply offer advertisers detailed reports on where, when, and how their effort to engage fell short. Or you might choose to partner with the advertiser and use the proprietary data you have to co-create advertisements. From time to time the data might also be provided at a reduced fee or no charge at all as a reward to those who routinely bid on advertising instruments on the exchange.

Targeted Marketing Solutions

The detailed consumer profiles you construct based on exchange participation may be even more valuable to advertisers off the exchange. More specifically, the profiles a news outlet collects can be segmented and sold to advertisers who may want to connect directly with individual segments. However, great caution must be taken here so as not to violate the trust exchange participants have in your news outlet. First, exchange participants should be given an option as to whether they would like to receive tailored targeted marketing efforts. Allow them to determine whether they would like to participate and you will build trust. You will also create segments that are much more valuable to advertisers. These segments will have given their permission to be marketed to by advertisers. It means a direct pitch is more likely to be received favorably. Segments like these create valuable opportunities for advertisers. Conversely, your job is also to create value for those granting permission. It means you must demand advertisers provide a clear and valuable benefit in their marketing offer. Only after the advertiser agrees to offer a sample, discount, or free trial will the advertiser be entitled to market to this valuable segment. Each party benefits thanks, in part, to the connection your news outlet has made.

Strategic Communications Solutions

The data extracted from exchange participants in *The Pitch*

Store will allow your news outlet to help PR firms provide better service to their clients. Additional probing of exchange participants, after a benefit is offered, will produce qualitative data in regard to the effectiveness of a specific pitch. More importantly, the exchange provides news outlets with an opportunity to find out exactly why a news release, pitch, or alert was effective or not. The data is valuable to PR firms in a variety of ways. The data may be used to evaluate staff members creating pitches which may in turn help the firm reduce costs or become more efficient. It also empowers the firm to provide clients with new ways to target specific audiences in less obtrusive manners. The data you collect, so long as it is used respectfully, offers PR firms an opportunity to increase the value they provide clients.

I anticipate there'll likely be some who attempt to create a next generation news product entirely free to users. The temptation to offer all content for free will be great in light of all of the valuable data you'll be collecting and monetizing. However, I caution those who are tempted not to force models from a bygone era onto the future.

Remember, you are no longer selling the dead air in between content blocks. That degree of separation is quickly coming to an end. One day, it'll likely be gone for good. Today and in the future, advertisements will mingle with content in ways practitioners are just starting to experiment with.

Advertising as we know it will change even more dramatically than it has during the transition from desktop to mobile. Advertising will be data driven. It will increasingly become targeted, personalized, and beneficial to those at whom it is aimed. Advertisers will also have to show great restraint not to violate a target's trust, time, or special preferences.

The point is content producers must strike strategic partnerships with advertisers in ways not characteristic of bygone eras. If you believe content and advertising will converge in ways I outline you will not only understand the need to form partnerships but you will also want to steer how advertisers mingle with your content.

At stake is the relationship content creators have with content consumers. You certainly will not want to be perceived as allowing blatant interruptions by advertisers. Tacitly approving of obtrusive advertising will erode the trust consumers place in your organization. The manner in which advertisers behave will impact your reputation moreso than it has in the past.

You'll no longer be able to run a disclaimer telling consumers the advertisement doesn't necessarily reflect the station ownership's views. By allowing an advertiser access to your tribe you are associating your own reputation with that of the advertiser for better or for worse.

Advertisers are quickly learning there is less benefit today in interrupting content consumption. Digital natives will perceive interruptions much more harshly than those who grew up with advertising interruption as a way of life. Therefore, it is best to form solid partnerships with advertisers to create marketing materials that are not only highly personal and targeted but also distributed in the least obtrusive manner possible.

The trend has already begun.

The Google Maps update released in May 2013 is an example of content melding with advertising in a manner that creates value for all of the parties involved. Besides better location features and personalized Maps search results, Google is offering advertisers an opportunity to touch consumers like never before.

Savvy marketers will now be able to geofence their advertisements and target Maps users who may literally be right outside their store. Analysts say the Maps application Google has upgraded and linked with Google+ is the only true opportunity marketers currently have to seamlessly meld advertising with content.

Additional opportunities will sprout as blending proliferates.

What marketers aiming to seamlessly blend advertising with content are truly after is increased engagement. They'll want consumers to interact with their advertisement in some manner. That means the advertisement itself must contain premium content. It must not only be attractive in terms of grabbing attention but it must also contain content that viewers of your content find valuable.

This is why creating user profiles is so critical to future success.

If you're shaking your head in disbelief or your gut is telling you that what I describe is years away, at least for news outlets, I'd urge you to invest some time understanding the business model underpinning Tivo.

Besides providing a user interface that is valuable to consumers, Tivo's set-top boxes contain software that gathers information on which commercials are viewed and which are not. Tivo then combines this viewing data with purchasing data from the home and creates composites of which marketers once only dreamed.

The future is now.

Selling blocks of dead air to advertisers pushing a single message to the masses is a model on its death bed. It won't die quickly but it will die.

It means the first in the industry to overhaul the way it sells will be the first to establish meaningful relationships with advertisers. They'll begin making connections that last much longer than the thirty second ads of yesteryear.

Those who are first to embrace the concept of connection selling will have a head start in the race to reinvent themselves as relevant and profitable concerns in the future. It is only through reinvention that next generation news outlets will position themselves to make profitable connections.

These connections will be harder to establish than the simple selling taking place today. However, these connections will prove more valuable and have greater longevity than the advertising relationships of today.

Resist and become irrelevant.

Embrace and become indispensable.

The Transition

Who do you want to engage?
The answer to this question will dictate who you become, which direction you'll head as an organization, and how you'll get there.

The next generation news outlet will be forced to choose its audience. No longer will news outlets be able to survive trying to be all things to everyone. This is a strategy that ultimately ensures you wind up as nothing to anyone.

With few exceptions today's newscasts contain neither breadth nor depth. They are masters of no domain yet market themselves as if they are masters of all domains.

Appealing to the masses has caused many of us to become irrelevant to the niches. The result is many of these niches have left television news.

These niches, largely ignored by television news, have found they are valuable, relevant, and important. Online content creators are corralling the niches television news has ignored, discarded, or failed to invest in. These innovators recognize the value of the niche. They understand serving a niche can be both profitable and scalable.

Digital content creators are narrowly focused on their niche. In turn, that niche becomes extremely loyal to the content creator. A level of trust develops. A bond is forged. These are intangibles television news is unable to create and nurture due to its attention to the masses. Television news is unable or unwilling to focus narrowly on just one group. It fears doing so and believes ignoring the masses would result in lost advertising.

It would likely.

However, the digital shift in advertising is a signal some appear to be ignoring. Siemer & Associates calculates online ad spending grew 19% to $105 billion in 2012. That's approximately 20% of the total advertising spend. Estimates indicate online advertising will likely grow to one-third of the total ad spend over the next decade or so.

While traditional advertising isn't dead, it's certainly evolving. I've described the future in detail: targeted, highly personal, relevant, and valuable.

It will also be guided by neuroscience data as we continue to learn more about cognition and how marketers can use it to influence and persuade.

It's impossible to create advertising of this caliber and complexity for the masses, all at once, and expect it to be consumed at the exact time you say so. Technology has splintered the audience in too many ways to cling to convention and survive.

Advertising is headed toward specificity.

It's in our interest to beat advertisers to the punch.

The business model I've laid out will take time and money to build. It'll require courage to experiment, fail, and try again. It'll also require technical expertise to manage, sell, and leverage.

It will not be implemented overnight.

What starts as a side project, then offered in beta form to loyal first adopters, will not likely be rolled out in its entirety for some time.

However, as we work on building out the infrastructure of the future we must not stand still. We must begin the process of picking audiences, creating value for them, and incrementally moving them toward the next generation news product I've outlined.

None of this requires true innovation as does the exchange-based model of the future.

The job we are tasked with today requires incremental yet continuous change. We know where we're headed as far as a business model. How we get there is what news managers should be concerned with today and every day.

The key is to change our focus.

Remember, we are narrowing our perspective from one that is currently overly broad and adopting one that is much more narrow and specific. We must become the trusted best friend of a few rather than the popular buddy to everyone at the party.

We control who we attempt to befriend.

We are choosing a specialty much like a doctor might. This doesn't mean that suddenly the world is void of general practitioners. There'll always be a need for family physicians. However, it means we have the opportunity to become more valuable by choosing the audience we wish to please. Specialists make more money than general practitioners. They generally perform fewer procedures and see fewer patients than general practitioners. However, they are compensated at higher rates because of their specialty.

Choosing a specialty can be just as profitable for news outlets.

And choosing a specialty doesn't mean we must mourn the loss or ignore each and every other niche to which we might be attracted. Doctors with specialties often join forces and form their own hospitals that provide patients with a number of specialty procedures. Physician-owned hospitals are more profitable than general hospitals for a variety of reasons. I simply draw the comparison so you have an example on which to model your newsroom.

It's your job as a news director, general manager, or station owner to choose which niches you want to delight. However, picking an audience is much different than choosing graphics packages, set designers, or weather gear. Choosing an audience requires a deeper commitment. One that cannot be broken without hard feelings and negative publicity.

The choices made in one market will likely differ greatly in another. Choice will be influenced by a variety of elements including but not limited to:

- Geography
- Political preference
- Workforce composition

- Regional tastes
- Corporate headquarters
- Religious beliefs
- Income
- Attractiveness to advertisers
- Current staffing

Choosing niches to serve doesn't mean ignoring general news viewers. However, understanding the attitudes, beliefs, and behaviors of these viewers will quickly help you understand the limits of boxes, categories, and designations.

An individual included in one niche may also be a member of another niche. A general news enthusiast may also be a member of a particular niche. Niche crossover is the norm rather than the exception. It's why you must be mindful not to allow the existence of niches to blind you to crossover opportunities.

Labels simply allow us to better organize our lives. They should not, when we're talking about humans, be perceived as definitive, permanent, or constraining. Conversely, identifying niches allows us to serve them better. It enables us to create content with only them in mind.

Once we understand the role niches play in our transformation from a broad perspective to one that is much narrower in scope, we must consider how we create and provide content to these audiences. Not only are we transitioning to a next generation news product but so too are those interested in consuming the product.

So we must ask ourselves what incremental change looks like on a screen?

Remember, that screen may be in our living rooms, on our phones, on the lenses of our glasses, or inside a vehicle. How might we attract people to this transitional product? What characteristics might it include so that viewers engage and ultimately get lost in the offering?

Understand, the goal is to entice them so deeply they wind up lost.

Lost is the new found.

The New Anchor

Have you met the new anchor?

You know the questions that are asked inside a newsroom when a new anchor is introduced to the staff.

Is she pretty?

Is he tall?

Wonder how she'll gel with the others?

Do you think he's a prima donna?

The answer to each of the questions above is yes…

No…

And maybe!

With that, are you the news manager ready to meet the new anchor of your next generation news product?

Introducing…

The viewer.

That's right.

The viewer is now the new anchor.

The new anchor is much different from many of the old anchors. The new anchor is interested in quality content and expects to play a role in selecting what is covered and how it is covered. He's interested in choosing, shaping, and influencing the news product he and others see.

The new anchor is infinitely more concerned with the content than her hair and makeup. She might even read the content more than once. She might even question the veracity, tone, or relevance of a particular piece of content.

The not so subtle anchor jabs included here are not meant to offend, hurt, or ridicule anyone who for some reason might feel targeted. I'm simply illustrating the difference in mindset news managers must adopt if they are to be successful in their transition.

Every decision you make must take into account the new anchor's point of view. Obviously, the new anchor's consumption patterns will ultimately determine what is covered, how it is covered, and when it is covered. However, it is more complicated than that.

How a news outlet designs its screen will center around functionality, simplicity, and navigational ease. Each change, tweak, or alteration will be made to improve the new anchor's experience.

The era of pandering to your two main anchors is over.

Now your job is to please your many anchors.

You're tasked with giving them the reigns.

The consumer is now, in essence, the anchor of his or her own newscast. It means you'll be required to arrange each of their home screens with a variety of options that'll allow them to personalize their experience.

But how does it look?

Ultimately, each home screen will be customizable. Preferred content will flow to the forefront based on a user's stated preferences and according to a user's prior engagement history.

But before we delve deeper into the customized world we've signed up for by choosing niches, we must conceive the very first experience a user might have with our news product. Before they can customize or create usage histories, they will first experience a start screen of our design and choosing. I'll leave the details to the artist. However, the foundation on which the product is built must be based on choice.

Providing viewers with choices, layers, and options is key.

You may have noticed throughout the book how I've given readers the option of jumping forward to another section without first reading the one in front of them. I stole the concept from fiction writers of the 1980s.

Do you remember them?

They were often referred to as "Choose Your Own Adventure" books and they weren't just game books. They allowed readers to decide which path a protagonist took when confronted with a life-altering decision. The books had multiple endings depending on which path a reader elected to take. It forced readers to become involved and required reader engagement.

The concept was well ahead of its time.

But now it's enjoying a bit of a revival online.

Movie makers are now posting choose your path videos on YouTube. The idea is to involve the viewer in a way that dictating a storyline does not. Obviously, some people would prefer a seat on grandpa's lap and be told a complete story without having to make decisions along the way.

I'm not advocating news outlets give up editorial control within a news story. What I am suggesting is that you allow viewers to choose their own path while simultaneously not ignoring those who would prefer not having to engage in this manner.

Both are possible to accomplish.

The next generation news product, during transition, will produce a more traditional broadcast available to those who prefer the news outlet set the agenda, stack the show, and offer the content in the order it prefers.

However, the next generation news outlet must also offer a "choose your path" option. One where viewers can build their own newscasts, order them according to their preferences, or simply view individual pieces of content.

It is similar to a restaurant buffet where consumers pick and choose what they want. Should they find something they like they are welcome to help themselves to more. When they come across something they do not like they are not forced to consume it.

You are the server.

Your job is to set the buffet line. Offer an array of choices. Replenish those that are consumed most heavily. And replace those that are not consumed with something you believe will be more appetizing.

Each choice a consumer makes provides you with an additional piece of data.

The platform beneath the content you offer for free must include software attributes similar to that of an editing timeline or a rundown. This is where consumers can pick, choose, and arrange the content they want to see.

They will have the choice to consume pieces of content individually. Or they can build their own rundown, sit back, and watch the stories they have chosen.

However, those who want the ability to personalize or build their own newscast will likely be required to log in. You'll likely already have much of their personal data as many will likely be consuming your content via the application they downloaded, agreeing to your terms of service.

This is why news outlets must not skimp in regard to the content they offer for free. They must routinely post high value content, or at least portions of it, in an effort to attract people to check in with the outlet. While still free, the data a consumer generates when personalizing a newscast is the price they will pay for the opportunity. This data is the basis for the additional revenue streams outlined earlier.

It's also important to make sure you allow the new anchor to decide when they consume your product. Kicking back and watching the newscast the viewer has built is one option. However, many exist.

A viewer may also choose to partially sample a story and consume the rest of it later. They may fast forward or select stories out of order in relation to how they are arranged on the viewer's timeline. Or their behavior may combine a bit of both of the scenarios I just described.

It's why allowing viewers to store their selections is imperative. I'm referring to a news outlet's obligation to allow viewers to store in the cloud the news product they sample or the newscasts they create. This allows viewers to carry the content they've selected or personalized with them wherever they go. It allows them access regardless of time or place.

Cloud pricing has been commoditized. The cloud is where content will live in the future. It's what will allow viewers to access your creations anywhere. It is also how you'll combat the fact that digital natives grew up without appointment viewing.

More important though is where you will draw the line between free content and that which costs money.

I argue a subscription-based model based upon preferred niches and consumption histories, at least for a portion of your audience, will likely prove effective. You currently have a front row seat to how popular subscriptions become as Google is now offering subscriptions to a number of YouTube channels. The experiment will help teach us whether people will be willing to pay for content on a site where it has always been free. The parallels are obvious.

However, I realize television news will likely experiment with a variety of paywall structures just like the newspaper industry is doing. In fact, the micropayment model some newspapers are experimenting with has the potential to evolve into an exchange-based model.

How you charge for premium content in the near future or during the transition is outside the scope of this book. However, I urge news outlets to employ a variety of pay-for-content models simultaneously. Tailoring each model to the preference of the niche is the key to succeeding.

Niches may differ in how they prefer to pay for content. Because you are constructing a highly social news product you're likely to learn quickly how niche audiences prefer to consume premium content.

Some might want to prepay.

Others may want to subscribe.

Some might prefer to pay as they go.

I urge news managers not to force their preferred pay models onto discerning niches. One size no longer fits all. You're not broadcasting to the general mass. You must take into account differing tastes, preferences, and leanings.

Newspapers are forcing single pay models upon their digital audiences. Besides treating their niches as faceless masses, I argue newspapers are leaving money on the table. For instance, people consuming the sports section are likely to feel much differently about paying for content than those who first consume the lifestyle section. If you're skeptical just look at the reasons Disney cites in considering whether to subsidize the data plans of those who routinely consume streaming content from its ESPN website.

Providing choices will empower your viewers.

It will also likely make them more attractive to advertisers.

Above all else though, the transitional business model must be created and maintained in an environment where failure in pursuit of higher margins is applauded. The key is failing quickly. Fail quickly and move on to the next tweak in the model.

The people responsible for the model will undoubtedly need the freedom to make errors so long as those errors are recovered from quickly and with only a minor loss of capital.

Incremental innovation is the key to progress.

Bet the company risk taking will lead many to fail.

Creativity, inventiveness, and ingenuity will ultimately drive success in terms of developing a business model for your transitional product.

No matter how you structure the model it's important to create content that illustrates the importance of your premium content. These illustration pieces will be offered for free on the content buffet. Not only might they provide another opportunity in terms of advertising but they also provide an opportunity for news outlets to convert nonpaying consumers into paying consumers.

You might also experiment with guest passes so nonpaying consumers can sample your premium content for a period of time. It may also pay dividends to offer premium content for free to certain viewers on occasion. Again, you are only limited by your creativity in terms of how you structure your paywall.

Please do not dismiss crowdfunding either.

While many may believe crowdfunding is a new concept in terms of news, it's not. National Public Radio is the pioneer of crowdfunding. It was crowdfunding before it was cool. NPR stations jump on the air and practically beg for money four times a year. They are the original crowdfunders despite already being subsidized by taxpayers.

The problem is public radio has failed to innovate. These stations give away mugs and t-shirts as incentives to donate. It's the way they've done it for years. And it's the way they do it today. While successful thus far, it's not clear whether these types of incentives will ultimately resonate with digital natives.

Why not innovate in terms of crowdfunding?

Why not tell your crowd that if it meets a certain funding goal everyone who chipped in gets to watch the piece for free?

You might also create a tiered system in which the size of the donation dictates the package of content the donor ultimately receives. For instance, the project may be packaged with additional related content for those donating the most money. Or those at the top of the pledging tier may be entitled to see the content first, participate in the creation of the content in some manner, or otherwise receive related bonus content.

Crowdfunding is also an opportunity to bring back the investigative units that have been cut from stations around the country.

It will not likely be successful in every market. But news outlets that find themselves with niches attracted to longer form investigative pieces now have the opportunity to fund those pieces in ways not possible in the past.

News outlets now have the opportunity to explain to viewers how time and labor-intensive true investigative reporting really is. Afterward, news outlets might lay out a dozen investigative story ideas people may be interested in seeing you execute. Outlets may also post popular investigative tips a niche might be interested in seeing come to fruition.

It'll be a news manager's job to calculate how much money is needed to gather, write, edit, and earn a profit on the investigative stories under consideration. Once a dollar figure has been determined it is the crowd that will decide which projects, if any, to fund.

You might also creatively partner with sponsors to revive investigative journalism.

For instance, the project rules may state that if a crowd were to fund the project well before the funding deadline...

Or if there was so much interest in a given project it was overfunded by a specific amount...

Then by default a participating sponsor would step in and fund the project itself. In the event this happens, every member of the crowd that originally funded the project gets their money back and gets to view the project for free.

I'm certain some of you have ethical concerns.

However, Charlie Rose has been balancing corporate sponsorship with in-depth journalism for decades and so can you.

But only if you really want to.

I've been a broken record throughout this book in regard to noting how only your creativity can limit how you structure the next generation news product. Similarly, you will only be limited by your ethical boundaries in regard to the sponsorship of investigative reporting.

There's nothing to prevent a news outlet from contributing to a crowdfunded project as well. In fact, a news organization making the first contribution signals it's just as committed as those in the crowd.

A popular reporter might even be the first donor. Despite massive reporter salary cuts, turn to page 161 to find out why you're overpaying the majority of your reporters.

Local news outlets simply do not have access to the philanthropic entities currently funding larger scale investigative projects. The possibilities are seemingly endless in terms of how news outlets fund their own larger projects in the future.

It's backward compared to how content is created now.

But imagine knowing in advance how many viewers you'll have for a particular piece. Imagine knowing this prior to the piece airing, much less being completed. It's a complete reversal from the present day model. But it is one that, at the very least, is worth exploring as a possibility as your news outlet transitions.

Below are ideas, strategies, and tactics to be considered for inclusion in transitional news products:

Stop Breaking News
At least during traditional newscasts. Break news as soon as you can. Distribute breaking news via every channel at your disposal. Withholding news from a devoted tribe is a surefire way to breed mistrust. Additionally, when you routinely break news outside your traditional newscast you drive people to your traditional newscast. If you are offering viewers the opportunity to build their own newscasts why would you place breaking news only in the newscast you produce? It may go unconsumed by many who regularly

consume the individual pieces of content you create. Each time you break news outside a traditional newscast you also create an opportunity to push those who consume it toward a newscast you produce. Traditional newscasts are where you supplement, layer, and highlight nuances you were unable to immediately after breaking the news. By reserving breaking news for only your traditionally produced newscast you are hiding it from people not currently watching your traditional newscast. However, when you break news on Twitter, Facebook, YouTube, in the morning, on weekends, and after hours you expose your organization to crowds that are not currently paying attention to you. Intentionally breaking news outside your traditional newscast gives people a reason to begin watching your newscast.

Socialize Criticism

You've received countless calls, letters, and emails from irate viewers. News managers are often successful in remedying situations that start out highly turbulent. Often, these situations are resolved in peaceful and satisfactory manners. It's high time we incorporate this into our transitional news product. Invite criticism. Meet it face to face. The more social we make our news product the more people are likely to participate in or engage with our product. We should no longer hide viewer complaints or kudos. Bring all of it public. Loyal tribe members are likely to come to your defense when an irate consumer is being unfair or is uninformed. The power of the crowd will ultimately rest in your favor if you're doing the kind of work we originally got into this business to do. So make the criticism public. Invite the critics to participate. News managers know the critics are often satisfied just by being heard. They don't believe you're listening. They don't believe you care. And that angers them. However, you will not only show them you're listening and care but you can also show the world when you socialize the criticism you receive.

Reverse the Push

Many of you are executing counter to how you should be. Countless times I've seen newsroom staffers push newscast viewers to the web. In reality, this is backward and far less lucrative than the contrary. Newscast ratings are dwindling. It means we are pushing an ever decreasing number of viewers to our websites. Eventually, we're going to run out of people to push to our websites. What we should be doing is building a digital base and pushing them to our newscasts. If you believe even a quarter of what I've outlined thus far you understand you must have a web first mentality. Ignore the television broadcast, at least initially, and begin stories online. Break news first on the web. Begin investigative pieces on the web. And hatch general assignment reports first on the web. When you start online you create an opportunity to ask everyone there to follow you to the traditional newscast you've produced. When you deliver value online and socially and offer additional value inside your traditional newscast you drive people to a newscast they otherwise are not likely watching. It's counterintuitive, just like breaking news everywhere but your newscast, unless it's unavoidable. But once you build loyalty online it should not end there. You should leverage the loyalty you create and lead people to a traditionally produced newscast where they can consume the conclusion of the piece they originally began consuming online. Or at least more of it.

Instead of an anchor saying, "For more on this go to our website…" your anchor should be saying, "It's a story that began on our website and now we know even more…"

Hang Your Mistakes

And hang them even higher than your staunchest critics might. News outlets must begin policing themselves better than they are currently. They should want to be first to point out mistakes, shortcomings, and questions that should've been asked in their news product. If you make a mistake publicly you need to ask for forgiveness publicly. A self-policing news outlet builds credibility and authority not afforded others who lack the courage to do so. The return of the newspaper ombudsman might just be what television news needs to restore the credibility survey after survey says it has lost. The television ombudsman will initiate investigations on behalf of consumers who feel they've been wronged, underserved, or ignored. Her investigations may include confronting and asking tough questions of reporters, producers, and news managers. The ombudsman will have the authority to be harshly critical of the news outlet. I'm certain your legal team is cringing right now and urging you to ignore this part of the book. But there are consequences outside courtrooms. And nowhere should those consequences be greater than internally. If we do not dramatically improve the way we hold ourselves accountable we are likely not long for this world as a going concern. Again, socializing the role of the ombudsman will only serve to draw us closer to those we aim to delight. Hangings were public for a reason. Hanging your mistakes publicly will yield rewards for those brave enough to be vulnerable in front of their viewers.

Subprime Weekends

Weekend news products are often subprime. Just like the toxic mortgage securities that nearly crashed the entire financial world in 2008, the toxic newscasts stations broadcast on weekends are not doing them any favors. The majority of stations are 5 day a week operations. Skeleton crews often produce hours of weekend newscasts and are willing to fill the time with whatever they run across. If you're only going to do your best 71% of the week then close up the shop on weekends. Cut your operating costs and tell whoever is left among your viewers you'll see them at the start of the following week. There are plenty of reasons to treat a Saturday different from a Monday. However, none of them are acceptable if your goal is to be the best. Broadcasting a subprime weekend newscast tarnishes the product you put out during the week. Viewers do not separate the weekday product from the weekend product. Neither should you. Imagine if news outlets were honest with their audiences. Imagine starting a newscast by saying any of the following:

- It's Friday night and that means the B-team is on the case
- Not many of you watch on Saturday so that's why we're skimping
- It's Sunday morning and we have nothing new, so enjoy the Saturday night re-rack

Fire your weekend crews, save the money, and run nothing but infomercials on weekends if you're not going to treat weekends like any other day of the week. You're only hurting yourself by faking it on weekends. A little planning during the week can make you shine on the weekend. Working all week so you can create a fantastic Sunday piece will position you as a market leader. Your competition will be at a disadvantage. They won't be able to confirm on a Sunday what you've been working all week. Weekends are springboards that allow stations to earn a head start for the week ahead. Your competitors will start the week chasing you. Meanwhile, you'll be advancing what you broke or onto something else. Or you can continue creating a subprime news product and risk additional viewership collapse. Your choice.

A transitional news product must not be mistaken for anything more permanent. It should never be pronounced as done, complete, or finished. Even successful transitional news products must continue to evolve if they are to achieve long-term success.

It is a news manager's responsibility to create an environment that rewards experimentation, failure, and reinvention. Those clinging to convention will only reduce the speed at which a newsroom's transitional product becomes a next generation news product.

I've spent much of the book attempting to strip readers of the assumptions, clichés, and conventional wisdom that have eroded the credibility of television news. I've spent an even greater amount of time proposing an alternative news product structure designed to earn today's broadcast news operations a spot in the digital future.

However, much of what I've outlined is likely to fail unless the industry regains its respect for premium content.

Even if a news manager were to implement everything I've outlined thus far plugging in the same content you're producing today would only result in failure. The structure I've outlined simply allows you an opportunity to distribute your content. It does not entitle you to success. The business model described thus far only provides you with a chance to succeed.

The next generation news product will be judged by the quality of its content.

Only those willing to dedicate themselves to producing the highest quality content should consider investing in the infrastructure I've described. Without premier journalism a news outlet will not build an audience worthy of the investment necessary to build what I have outlined.

Premium journalism must be admired above all else.

It must be revered more than the platform, marketing, or distribution that allows it to be consumed.

It's not enough to fall in love again with journalism.

We must walk up to her, extend our hands, and ask her out. We must take the risk others are unwilling to take.

While many profess their love for journalism most are not practicing it. Most are not true to the one they say they love. In fact, the majority spend more time covering their tracks and hiding the shortcomings of their commitment.

Only those who find the courage to ask her out again will be granted an opportunity to prove their love is real.

Journalism isn't a jilted lover.

She gives second chances.

But only to those willing to commit to the hard work this relationship requires.

The Lonely Reporter

I was a lonely reporter.
Rarely did I bump into reporters from competing stations.

This was by design. I didn't want to see another reporter while I was working. In fact, this is one way I measured success.

If I routinely saw other reporters covering the same story on which I was working I knew I wasn't working smart or hard enough. Conversely, I knew that not seeing competitors for a prolonged period of time meant I was succeeding where they were not.

At times I'd work months without seeing another reporter.

Adopting this mentality is both scary and stressful. It requires a commitment others are not willing to make. It also means holding yourself to a higher standard.

It's also rare.

The majority of television news reporters are not hunters.

They're spoon-fed and content with being handed an assignment. They're hooked on and survive on a form of content welfare that has become pervasive in newsrooms. More specifically, they are dependent upon someone else to provide them with what they need to survive as a reporter.

This isn't entirely bad.

News of the day must be covered. A newsroom needs reporters who can take what is handed to them, quickly comprehend it, and deliver it concisely on live television. Most reporters are competent in this regard.

Problems only arise when reporters begin to rely on being handed an assignment.

When they expect the station to provide them with news.

Continuing to feed a reporter in this manner only reinforces their behavior. Repeatedly feeding reporters creates a newsroom packed with takers rather than givers. It's what ultimately turns your news product into a commodity. Each station winds up covering the same stories, at the same time, in relatively the same way.

The reporters may look different but the content does not.

Instead of remedying the underlying problem the industry attempts to conceal its blemish.

How so?

Reporters compensate by attempting to make their live shots more active and lively than competitors on the same story. A nugget of information is intentionally left out of the reporter's story and given to an anchor to distribute so he or she might appear more involved in the story. Or we break up the original hand out and split it between two reporters and market it as important enough to deserve team coverage.

The only true remedy is a change in mentality.

You want reporters who desire to be lonely on your team.

Filling your newsroom with hunters is the only way to truly differentiate your product and create a competitive advantage. An environment must be created in which reporters are competing against one another for the right to do their own unique stories. Hunters cut from this cloth will view being handed a news of the day assignment as evidence their idea did not stack up favorably against those of newsroom competitors.

Hunters receive news of the day assignments reluctantly.

It's not that they won't execute a news of the day assignment competently or better than the competition. It's simply a sign they did not win the idea race of the day. In fact, the best use it as motivation to find something more unique and compelling the following day.

Reporters producing true works of journalism will not routinely run into reporters from other news outlets. They are headed in a direction others are not. It is not a well-traveled path. However, it is one everyone will aspire to take, but only after it is exposed by the leader.

"I skate to where the puck is going to be, not where it has been."

-Wayne Gretzky

News bosses certainly talk a good game on this front. Reporter job listings and news directors generally require that reporter candidates:

- Enterprise story ideas
- Routinely break news
- Force the competition to play catch up

The problem is these job requirements have become clichés. And clichés make for lousy objectives and job requirements. Why is this?

Almost every reporter is told she is required to achieve the aforementioned goals. However, few are held accountable in real time. More specifically, seldom are there consequences for reporters who fall short of these goals in the short-term. Only at the end of a reporter's contract is he generally confronted with the shortcomings of his performance.

By then it's too late.

Time and money have been wasted.

But what if the problem is bigger than just the reporter?

What if you've set the wrong goals for your reporters?

How many of your reporters can thoroughly articulate what it means to enterprise or break news? Everyone knows intuitively what these terms mean in a newsroom context. But how many can thoughtfully define these terms in-depth?

Better yet, how many are routinely executing in accordance with these criteria?

Answering these questions will likely answer the most important: when is the last time you broke news? Understand first what does not count:

- Getting a victim's picture no one else has
- Interviewing a crying mother no one else interviewed
- Being first to broadcast what everyone else has

I'm asking about substantive, original, and impactful content that results in action, change, or differentiation.

When is the last time you really broke news?

If your answer is anything other than yesterday your newsroom likely lacks the reporting horses you need to win the news derby.

The majority of news managers have no metrics in place to objectively determine how often their reporters break premium news content. It is not substantiated, tracked, or analyzed.

No one is keeping track of the currency in which we should be trading.

Is there any other industry that does not measure progress, or lack thereof, in regard to its most important function?

One reason for this is that news managers often overestimate how often they actually break news. A variety of reasons are to blame for this. But adopting an objective means of measuring the quantity and quality of news you break will undoubtedly help news managers avoid this pitfall.

Establishing a newsroom of journalistic hunters who eat what they kill requires news managers to strip those overseeing newscasts of the lemming mentality. In other words, those determining what is covered must opt out of the herd and refrain from coverage simply because the competition is covering something.

You'll handcuff your hunters if you're constantly rerouting them to another news event simply because the event is being covered by other news outlets. This doesn't mean you don't cover newsworthy events. What it does mean is that you must reevaluate how you cover stories around which competitors swarm. Events once covered as packages may not actually require the presence of a reporter.

A news outlet dedicated to creating premium news content must attempt to preserve the gathering of that content without interruption. If the new goal is to send reporters to find and retrieve premium news content where no one else is looking it'll require sacrifice elsewhere. It'll require news managers to quell the initial reaction they have to break reporters when an unexpected news event occurs or when the competition breaks into programming with an item of which you aren't immediately concerned.

Lemmings, copycats, and those with a herd mentality will not likely perform well in a newsroom narrowly focused on going places others are not. Therefore it's important that those who oversee daily newscasts revere premium news content just as your reporters do. Without a like-minded support team your team of hunters will be turned into a disappointed band of gatherers.

Successful next generation news outlets must have the courage to lead and the discipline not to chase.

When you commit to going where the news will be rather than where it currently is you'll position your organization as a leader among its peers. This mentality will also serve you well on those rare occasions when reporters have no choice but to bump into other reporters.

For instance, years ago when a well known southern lawmaker died after spending decades in office I crowded in next to dozens of other reporters from across the country to cover the lawmaker's funeral.

Instead of packaging the parade, funeral, and reaction from fellow lawmakers my photographer and I went where no one else did. For instance, we told the story of the man tasked with digging and preparing the beloved lawmaker's cemetery grave. It was a job being done with urgency as the grave digger could hear the funeral procession getting closer and closer.

It was an interview, story, and connection with viewers no one else created that day. It allowed us to differentiate ourselves from the competition. We were the only outlet offering viewers something they couldn't find anywhere else.

Reporters at crowded scenes who look behind them are often handsomely rewarded.

Filling your newsroom with reporters itching to go where no one else is also requires news managers to change how they hire reporters.

In fact, the hiring process must be reversed.

Right now, the majority of news managers only evaluate reporter candidates when they have a vacancy. They post the job, wait for the links and demo reels to come in, and then engage in that infamous 15 second per demo reel viewing they're known so well for.

It's a shotgun approach to hiring and one that leads to less than optimal hiring decisions.

Instead, news managers should adopt a rifle approach to hiring reporters.

A continuous, specific, and targeted hiring process will yield better results than the one currently in practice. Like the reporters you're interested in hiring, you must adopt a hunter's mentality. This requires looking when you're not obligated to do so. When you don't have a job opening.

News managers who routinely look for reporters when they do not have to are more apt to find reporters who are on the prowl for stories when and where their peers are not. News managers with a short list of reporters create head starts for themselves against those who are beginning the hiring process cold.

Targeting impressive reporters also eliminates the urgency and time constraints often present when news managers are making hiring decisions. The luxury of time when evaluating reporters reduces the mistakes often made in a hurry.

A cliché job listing posted to the masses is likely to yield that which is similar to what is sown. While a unique, thoughtful, and intentionally time-consuming hiring process will not produce a large pool of quality candidates, it will identify a unique few who comprise the cream of the crop.

Aggressively pursue the best.

The hiring process is your opportunity to set an example.

The hiring process is also one in which it is highly important to be cognizant of the niches you have chosen to serve. The niches you're attempting to delight will dictate where and how you begin the hiring process. It might also lead you in directions you hadn't previously considered.

More specifically, a next generation news product built exclusively on the creation of premium news content will require a hiring mechanism not currently in practice.

You'll be hiring solely based on content creation.

Not hair, cute smiles, or tight tops.

We know anyone with a smartphone and a connection can broadcast themselves to the world now. This has resulted in viewers becoming increasingly desensitized to performance, personal appearance, and on air presence.

That's not to say these attributes aren't important, relevant, or valuable. It simply means the viewing public now places a lesser degree of importance on these attributes, in terms of news dissemination, than it once did.

Digital natives are often described as more accepting, inclusive, and willing to embrace diversity in its many forms than prior generations. With this in mind it should be clear next generation news managers will have much more discretion in terms of who they hire and why. Gone are the days of excluding a candidate based solely on aesthetics.

The key will be to find and hire those who create content that creates value.

Achieving this may also require taking a page from Silicon Valley.

The best and the brightest there rarely go to work for someone in the traditional sense. At least not initially. Instead, they start up their own companies and attempt to create something of value.

This has left many of the largest and well known companies in an uncomfortable position. Apple, Google, and

Yahoo understand they are not likely attracting the best and brightest during the hiring process. They realize the candidates they really want to hire are not applying for work at these large companies.

Why would they?

They're busy starting their own.

It's why large companies like the ones mentioned have begun acquiring startup companies. In many cases, the acquirers are not interested in buying the product, service, or technology the target has created.

Instead, the acquirers are interested in acquiring the target's founders as employees. These acquisitions often include terms requiring the target's founders to continue working at the acquiring company for a period of time to receive the full buyout price.

It's an expensive way to acquire talent. But it's one that illustrates the necessity of having top talent on your team.

It's also a model next generation news outlets may adapt or adopt.

Bloggers, podcasters, or newsletter maestros serving your market or niche may be attractive acquisition targets. If acquisitions are not possible, at least consider mutually beneficial partnership opportunities.

Regarding aesthetics, you'll quickly learn many of these thought leaders who have built massive followings and extremely loyal tribes are not likely to wind up on the cover of a magazine.

It simply reinforces the aesthetic desensitization underway and the notion that premium content trumps all else.

Identifying, hiring, or acquiring content creators for a next generation news product are prerequisites for building a successful content exchange. But what about your current staff?

These are the people on whom you'll rely for a transitional product.

The majority of these reporters are not lonely reporters. They gladly accept handouts. They are part of the herd. In fact, the majority lack the skill set necessary to go where others are not.

However, you can teach your reporters to be lonely.

To do so news managers must first upend how they think about their reporting staffs. Instead of having a staff full of general assignment (GA) reporters, a few of whom can also turn investigative pieces, news managers will create more value for viewers by creating a staff of subject specialists.

Right now news managers perceive reporters on their staffs as generalists, or utility players who can be plugged into any situation and produce competently. This model must be reversed if you aim to serve the niches you've chosen better than competitors.

A successful next generation news product will be produced by a staff of investigative reporters, all of whom can also complete general assignments if need be. This model stands in stark contrast to the current one.

The model I'm outlining raises the bar in terms of quality.

Rather than having a staff of generalists who lack specific expertise and asking them to produce investigative, long form, or in-depth pieces on occasion, a next generation newsroom will house a reporting staff that routinely produces investigative, long form, and in-depth pieces and is also capable of producing general assignments on occasion.

You're assembling or creating an all-star team.

While stars are capable of completing general assignments doing so is not why you chose them to be on your team. Stars are chosen because they perform a key function at a level exponentially higher than their peers. It's a news manager's job to ensure that's what stars spend the bulk of their time doing.

Certainly some of you are concerned about how this model will impact your news organization's cost structure. If you're concerned recruiting, hiring, or creating all-stars will negatively impact your organization's profitability, please jump ahead to page 161 and learn why you're mistaken.

Free agency is certainly not the only way to build a team of all-stars. I wrote earlier news managers are capable of creating a staff of lonely reporters as they build out a transitional news product.

A model exists to accomplish just that.

A Model Reporter Model

The Content Creation & Distribution Model identifies and combines the underlying components vital in the creation of premium content. It's a multilayered structure designed to ensure reporters are properly engaged in the necessary prerequisites of a next generation news product.

It's certainly not all inclusive.

However, it does provide a foundation often lacking in today's reporters.

Take a look.

The Content Creation & Distribution Model

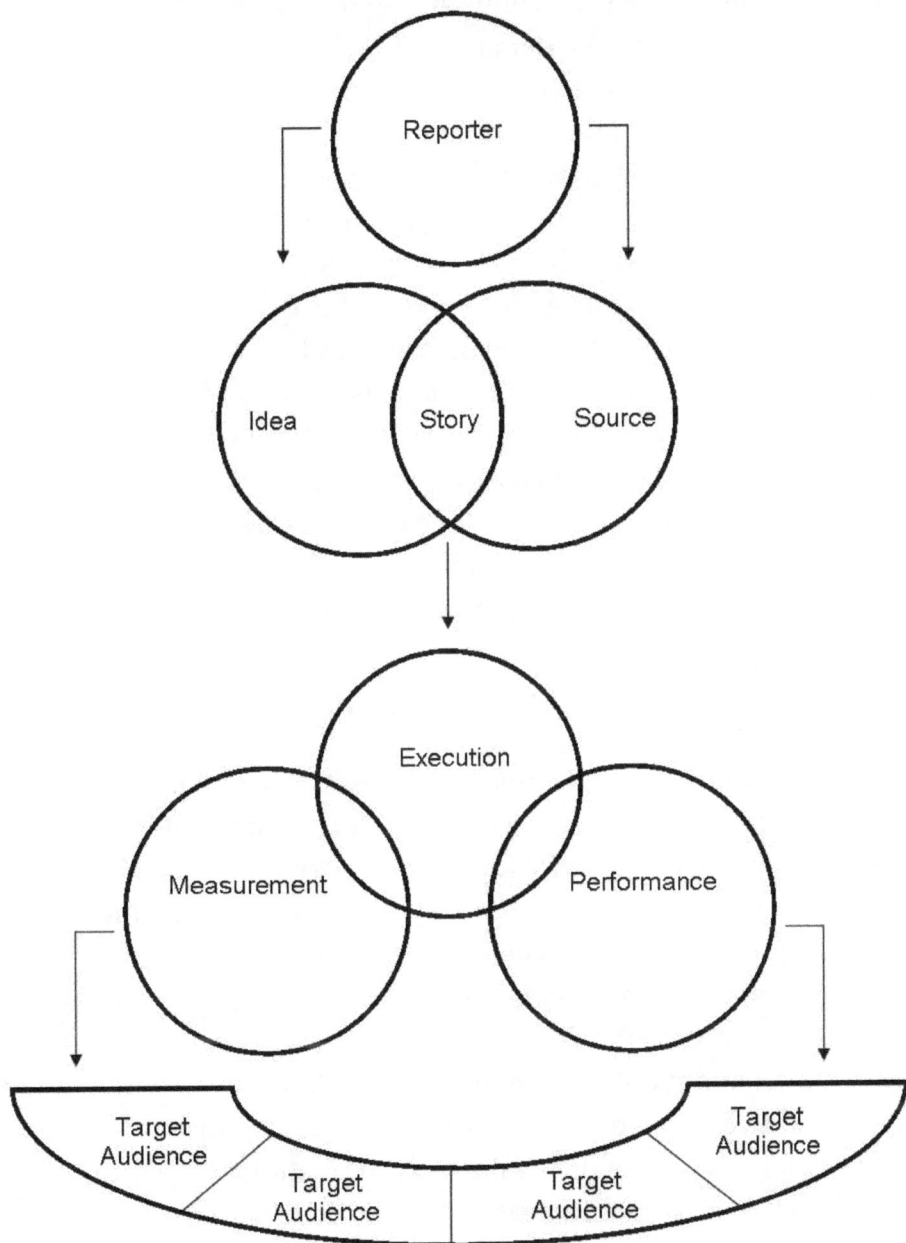

Reporter

Idea   Story   Source

Execution

Measurement   Performance

Target Audience

Target Audience

Target Audience

Target Audience

Reporter

Identifying and exploiting the assumptions, clichés, and conventional wisdom inherent in potentially newsworthy topics, events, or decisions will differentiate your work. Time constraints and the demands of multiple news shows often require reporters to take the status quo at face value and report it as fact. However, those who make the time and put forth the effort to probe more deeply will routinely uncover news competitors miss. The majority of television news produced today reinforces the status quo. A journalist's job is to poke holes in the status quo. Counterintuitive insight is newsworthy and fresh. The goal is to violate norms, boundaries, and expectations if warranted. However, gathering content of this magnitude requires a rebel-like mentality in terms of accepting what is being offered. Adopting what some call a "document state of mind" positions a reporter to fight words with facts. It also ensures a reporter is routinely receiving the bounties of records requests.

Source

The transient nature of the television news business makes source creation rare. Lazily relying on public information officers amplifies the void. However, properly structured newsrooms create an environment where reporters can build sources quickly. This isn't often done via social media or inside the newsroom. It requires interpersonal engagement. It's a three step process that includes identification, cultivation, and maintenance. It requires identifying former office holders who know how systems, agencies, and bureaucracies operate. It requires the cultivation of relationships based upon mutual benefit. It also demands maintenance in the form of engagement during times in which the reporter is not seeking information. Human intelligence, or HUMINT, is valued above all others by CIA officers. It should be just as revered by reporters in newsrooms. Sources are not built as news managers and consultants often discuss. Sources are created from scratch. The CIA trains officers how to identify, cultivate, and maintain sources. Reporters must be trained to do the same.

Story Idea

Reporters and sources may both generate ideas independently of one another. However, ideas generated in concert provide the strongest foundations for premium content generation. Just like public relations staffers who routinely write ineffective news releases, sources often lack an appreciation for what is actually newsworthy. I'm not talking about the ideas sources present reporters with. I'm focused on the ideas, information, and tips sources never actually mention because they're not aware these items might be newsworthy. After creating a source, reporters have an obligation to train the source to understand what is newsworthy. Those who ignore this responsibility are leaving money on the table in the form of hybrid story ideas. Hybrid story ideas are the type most likely to become premium stories. They emanate from the sweet spot shared by reporter and source. However, the creation of hybrid ideas is only possible once reporters understand how to tease out the ideas sources are initially inclined not to share.

Execution

The manner in which a reporter gathers, frames, and executes a story communicates what words cannot. The choices you make during the execution process are direct reflections of who you are as a news organization. How you go about gathering elements, the tone used throughout, and the overall story structure offer news organizations an opportunity to blend in or stand out. Story structure is just as important as gathering the proper elements. However, news managers and consultants pay it little attention. Ordering the story properly is paramount. An ineffective story structure dramatically reduces the impact of even premium content. Structural mistakes are routine. Empty leads, buried leads, and file video starts are broadcast all too often. Genuinely original and effective storytelling is happening in only a handful of markets. That handful often enjoys better ratings than competitors. It's an advantage consultants often misidentify or mislabel as superior branding. In reality, it's superior execution.

Performance

After the majority of reporters stood still and stared into the camera, news managers required reporters to walk, talk, and move. Now that the majority of reporters are walking and talking, what's next? Walking and talking has become a commodity. It provides you no differentiation. However, news managers routinely mistake the ability to do so for journalistic talent. Performance ultimately determines the majority of reporter hiring decisions. Increasing a reporter's energy, hand gestures, and movement are generally compensation for less than premium content or execution. Understand a next generation news product will not be viewed in a vacuum. It will be consumed and compared alongside video that is more active, energetic, and emotive than any of your reporters will have the right to be.

Innovative performances in a next generation news product will serve only to build trust with viewers. Reporters might surprise, reveal, or unearth. They might also be static. Performance objectives for a next generation news product will be based entirely on providing value to the viewer. Performances that create value and ultimately trust are the only types of performances that will be sustaining.

Measurement

An objective means of measuring reporter performance has remained elusive in newsrooms. The best reporters in each shop are generally known. They stand out. But if you were to ask a news manager why a certain reporter stands out you'd likely be met with anecdotes, analogies, and examples. There's nothing inherently wrong with praising a reporter for her accomplishments. However, a more precise way exists for managers interested in removing the subjectivity in evaluating reporter performance. Creating the metrics necessary to measure and compare reporters is contingent upon the objectives you set as an organization, the niches you have chosen to serve, and the degree to which you've adopted an exchange-based model. A thorough measurement program will include viewer engagement, preference, and outcomes. However, news managers interested in objectively evaluating reporter performance now can get some ideas on page 161.

Notice first in the model the crossover between reporters and sources. The sweet spot that is clearly evident in the model is one today's television news consultants often miss. News managers and consultants routinely coach, critique, and criticize reporters as if they work in vacuums.

This type of coaching is incomplete.

It is also a disservice to the reporter and the organization paying for the coaching.

The majority of television news consultants focus on a single element rather than the composite illustrated in the model. The model included here illustrates how interdependent each aspect of the premium content creation process is.

Optimum success depends on successfully executing each aspect of the model. News managers and consultants might tell reporters to build sources for instance, but rarely do they show them how to do so. Likewise, television news coaches rarely focus on how to generate ideas, execute, and structure them as stories. Even fewer help organizations create metrics that objectively measure a reporter's performance.

Much of the coaching being conducted today is short on substance and long on style. Style, or performance, is extremely important hence its inclusion in the model. But in and of itself performance will not sustain a next generation news organization.

The model outlined here is narrowly focused on helping reporters generate and distribute the premium content required of a successful next generation news product. While narrow in scope, it is a comprehensive model that addresses the reporter as a whole. Not only does it create a framework for the generation and distribution of premier content, but it may also be used to teach reporters how to successfully execute each aspect of the model.

A deficit exists today.

It's a deficit that was born by not teaching reporters how to properly and successfully execute their behind the scenes duties. Television news has become so preoccupied with on camera performance and marketing it has grossly neglected the fundamental competencies needed as foundations for optimal performance and marketing.

It's a gap this model attempts to fill.

Most news managers ask their reporters to generate original ideas, create sources, and properly structure stories. Few reporters actually achieve the goals news bosses set. Hence the creation of a comprehensive model.

To perform and market yourself optimally you'll first have to shore up a reporter's back office competencies.

The Content Creation & Distribution Model helps train reporters to excel behind the scenes. This is the only way a reporter can reach and sustain his or her maximum potential in front of the camera.

Performance and marketing become infinitely easier to successfully execute once a news organization builds a solid foundation. Rather than using performance and marketing to compensate for lackluster ideas or content, the premium content your reporters produce will become marketable in and of itself.

The Source Genocide

News outlets routinely commit source genocide. The reporters who do create sources, break news, and boost viewership ratings generally leave for bigger markets and paychecks. The sources these reporters make are dead once the reporter who created them bolts for greener pastures.

In reality though, these sources are massacred in a type of journalistic genocide that must be halted if a news outlet is to retain any value its reporters create.

News outlets generally make no material effort to retain a reporter who shows interest in jumping to a larger market. This behavior is grounded in reality. Stations generally cannot match a larger market's pay increase or a reporter's desire to move up.

However, making little or no effort to retain top reporters should not be replicated in terms of the reporter's sources. Allowing a reporter to walk out the door without retaining some value from the sources the reporter has created is akin to watching those sources die and doing nothing to stop it.

It's source genocide.

The sources die with the reporter.

News managers can bemoan what might be perceived as a lack of loyalty on the part of the reporter. Or disdain the transient nature of the business and the pitfalls that come with it. Or news managers can acknowledge reality and proactively behave in a manner that will benefit both the reporter and the station he or she is leaving.

Reid Hoffman, who helped build PayPal and co-founded LinkedIn, laid out a framework in the June 2013 issue of the *Harvard Business Review* that news managers may adapt and use to stop the source genocide.

In *Tours of Duty*, Hoffman and co-authors Ben Casnocha and Chris Yeh argue mutual investment is how employers and employees can both benefit from a present day work environment characterized by habitual turnover. The article states:

"A workable new compact must recognize that jobs are unlikely to be permanent but encourage lasting alliances nonetheless. The key is that both the employer and employee seek to add value to each other. Employees invest in the

*company's adaptability; the company invests in the
employees' employability. Three simple policies can make
this new compact tangible. They are (1) hiring employees for
explicit "tours of duty," (2) encouraging employees to build
networks and expertise outside the organization, and (3)
establishing active alumni networks to maintain career-
long relationships."*

Lopsided contracts are the norm in terms of agreements
between news organizations and reporters. For example, I
once turned down a job because of a clause in a contract that
allowed the employer to reset my salary at any level the
employer wished, at any time the employer desired, and
without any prior notice.

If I were building a news organization from scratch I
wouldn't ask any of my reporters to sign a contract. And I
certainly wouldn't bar them from working at a competing
station.

Is there a worse way to begin a relationship?

What I would do is use incentives to create an environment
in which reporters wanted to stay rather than being forced to
stay. For some ideas on how to accomplish this turn to page
161.

The "tours of duty" Hoffman writes about are based on
trust and commitment but not permanence. It's a concept
from which news organizations might benefit. Hoffman
argues entrepreneurial employees, who often have higher
aspirations and are poaching targets, are often high
performers who create value for companies even if their
employment is temporary.

News organizations that embrace the transient nature of
the business and the limited time they're likely to retain top

talent can learn to squeeze more value from high performers than those attempting to force employees to agree to unfavorable terms.

News organizations that force reporters into lopsided contracts set the tone for what has the potential to become a relationship based on resentment rather than trust. A mutually beneficial relationship built upon a temporary commitment and specific objectives has the potential to create more value than a contractual arrangement in which the reporter is counting down the days until the end.

Hoffman's second concept, encouraging employees to build expertise and networks outside the organization, is one that allows news organizations to partner with reporters in the creation of sources. Organizations that value creating original content and breaking substantive news must invest in this outside work.

Adapting Hoffman's concept means news organizations are likely to benefit from creating an environment in which they facilitate the creation of reporter sources. Doing so not only positions reporters to break substantive news, but also positions the organization as a partner in the source creation process and lays a foundation for retaining sources after reporters leave. Sources created together via mutually beneficial "tours of duty" are more likely to remain loyal to organizations despite a specific reporter's tour ending.

Personally, I find the status quo advantageous.

I always pounced when a well connected reporter from a competing station announced his or her departure. It meant the reporter's sources were up for grabs. The opportunity to poach sources has a dual impact. It strips one organization of a source and helps the poaching organization exploit the coup.

Poaching is extremely harmful but preventable.

Additionally, the niches the organization chooses to serve will often dictate the kind of expertise reporters are encouraged to acquire outside the organization. However, those niches should not limit a reporter from seeking additional expertise. In fact, the freedom to experiment may identify a previously unknown niche or one currently being underserved.

However, it's Hoffman's third concept, establishing active alumni networks, that is likely to be most valuable to news organizations.

Source genocide is real. When a reporter leaves his or her sources often leave as well. So too does the institutional knowledge that reporter acquired. Yet news organizations do little or nothing to stop this brain drain from occurring. Most appear to be content starting over from scratch each and every time a reporter leaves.

Source handoffs generally lack longevity.

Rarely are they successful as sources, by default, have no relationship with the person to whom they are being handed off. While creating sources together is one way to preserve a source relationship despite a reporter departure, so too is an alumni network.

The goodbye party should not be the last a station hears from its alums.

How an organization organizes or coordinates an alumni network is not what's important here. Neither is the degree of formality, involvement of human resources departments, or the platform on which a network is leveraged and maintained.

What is important is maintaining a network that can be tapped for ideas, insight, and direction that'll help those taking the place of alums.

What other business allows its most prized employees to walk out the door and never be heard from again?

News operations smart enough to co-create sources, invest in their reporters, and help them find better career opportunities will be rewarded via alumni networks. A reporter may be gone, but thanks to a vibrant alumni network, that reporter can still create value for the employer. They can tell replacements where to look, who to talk with, and identify mistakes to avoid.

The turnover inherent in the industry must be embraced.

News managers that fight the phenomenon with lopsided contracts, ignore it, or feel helpless in terms of doing anything about it are mistaken. Part of your job in creating a next generation news product is making the organization a place from which reporters are proud to have worked.

Shooting stars are to be enjoyed while they are shooting.

Knowing ahead of time they're not to be caught will make life much easier when they fade.

Invite successful alumni to return for coaching sessions. Urge them to leave a list of story ideas they wish they had the time to execute. Have them introduce replacements to sources and contacts.

Tapping the network for criticism will create value as well. Ask your alumni all-stars what did not work, how they'd fix it, and where the fix should start. Crave this type of critique and learn from it.

However you choose to benefit from an alumni network stop the current practice of severing all ties with departing alumni. An engaged alumni network will reduce your cost per reporter (CPR- you are measuring for that, right?) and provide value long after they are gone.

It'll also help end the source genocide.

Treat Reporters like Prize Fighters

The best or most popular prize fighters are paid more than fighters on the undercard.

Why?

They attract a larger number of people to the arena in which they are fighting. They sell more merchandise than less popular or effective fighters. And they draw a larger pay per view audience than their counterparts.

The best and brightest are the fight game's bread and butter.

However, television news does not operate under the same logic. Instead, television news, and its ill-fated march toward homogeny, views reporters as commodities with little qualitative difference across markets. In many instances news bosses are actually correct.

Have a hole in your reporting staff? Almost any reporter will do. Simply plug them in and they'll churn out a product similar to the rest. The majority act and behave like they believe a reporter should.

As they gain experience, many become caricatures of themselves.

Walk like a duck…

Quack like a duck…

And you'll be a duck, right?

News directors have a strong crutch on which to lean when justifying their plug and play mentality regarding reporters. The supply-demand imbalance among reporters is significant. Despite declining wages, increased workloads, and subjective performance reviews J-schools continue to churn out large numbers of reporters.

In turn, reporter salaries have declined in lockstep with viewership ratings and advertising revenue.

Authentic pride, which young, egotistical, and hedonistic reporters often lack, is generally the only thing that might motivate reporters in a newsroom. Aside from personal pride, newsrooms have done almost nothing to create incentives for reporters to break out.

This is fundamentally dissimilar to nearly every other business operating successfully today.

I'm certain news directors reading this far believe I'm bemoaning the dramatic reduction in wages the majority of reporters earn. In fact, the contrary is true.

News directors are overpaying the majority of their reporters.

Even at the stunningly inexpensive salaries you're paying reporters most are not earning what they receive or generating much of a return. The majority produce nothing proprietary. They do not break news. They do not routinely enterprise.

The majority are not hunters who eat what they kill.

The majority must be spoon-fed.

The majority are hooked on a form of content welfare that newsrooms do little or nothing to dissuade. The only way to break the reporter welfare cycle is to completely overhaul how a reporter earns his or her pay. To do this a news director must create incentives that spur newsroom competition.

I'm not talking about $25 gift cards, peer recognition, or an extra day off.

Instead of gestures of goodwill, create real incentives. Create a framework in which reporter pay is tied to reporter performance.

In other words, treat reporters as prize fighters.

Those who make the most money for their station will be compensated accordingly. Those who perform at lower levels receive less pay. It's rather simplistic but it's contrary to the way reporters are currently compensated.

Creating financial incentives that tie pay to performance will result in a number of benefits for television news outfits.

First, it weeds out the true journalists from those posing as journalists. It creates a barrier to entry for those who simply want to be on television. News directors will be fooled far less often when interviewing reporters who understand their pay is tied to performance.

A reporter's behavior will change dramatically when they realize they'll no longer be paid regardless of performance. Linking pay to performance ensures your weakest links will eliminate themselves. It also guarantees you'll build a newsroom of hunters.

Creating financial incentives emphasizes personal responsibility. It also injects a much needed dose of objectivity into a profession currently governed by subjectivity.

When you create a set of ultra-specific, time-specific, and objective metrics by which to measure your reporters you remove much of the subjectivity inherent in the business today. Hiring decisions, performance evaluations, and critiques will become far less cumbersome when a transformed newsroom clearly understands the metrics by which it'll be objectively measured.

Do you want your station to become the Mecca of television newsrooms?

Imagine how your life as a news director might change when you are able to offer a reporter candidate an unlimited salary. Imagine telling them you're not going to cap their wages. Imagine the looks on their faces when they realize your station is a place where they can do quality work, not only of which they are proud, but also of which they can earn an unlimited income.

Care to guess what type of reporters will be applying for work at your station?

The more money they earn for the station the more money they earn themselves. Obviously, the data generated on the exchange will provide real time results and a basis for how you'll compensate reporters.

Understand it works both ways.

While you're not capping what they can earn you're also not guaranteeing a minimum wage either, legalities aside. Clearly, new reporters will be at a disadvantage as they will lack the sources your veterans possess.

It's why you must devise a hybrid wage platform in which a new reporter is initially granted a base salary of some type and allowed to earn a commission on work he or she produces that resonates with advertisers and viewers. The platform's base salary and commission structure will decay over time until the reporter is self-sustaining or no longer interested, or able, to work in your newsroom.

If you're concerned about creating a cutthroat newsroom where reporters may be tempted to sabotage one another to earn more money you might also consider tying one portion of a reporter's bonus to another reporter's performance.

It's how Warren Buffett doles out bonuses to his managers.

A portion of one manager's bonus is contingent upon the performance of another manager. It's a structure aimed at fostering cooperation.

Care must also be taken to balance quality with quantity. The reporters who best strike that balance will be those who are compensated most generously.

The UFC , or Ultimate Fighting Championship, provides an example.

While the promotion does sign fighters to contracts that stipulate the number of events in which a fighter must participate to earn the agreed upon salary (quantity), additional financial incentives exist each step along the way (quality).

For instance, in addition to earning a portion of his salary for each fight, a fighter also has an opportunity to earn bonuses for:

- Fight of the night
- Knockout of the night
- Submission of the night

Each of these bonuses is generally worth between $50-$65,000. At times a single fighter has received two bonuses on top of his salary. Those who perform in a superior manner, become crowd favorites, and prompt larger pay per view buys position themselves to negotiate more lucrative contracts after the current ones expire.

It's one reason the best and brightest in the fight game aspire to the UFC.

They control their financial destiny.

Their earnings are contingent upon their performance.

The most talented generate a financial windfall for their organization and themselves. Everyone wins. And everyone is motivated to continue getting better. There is no room for the weak, lazy, or undisciplined.

The incentives created by the UFC, which is experiencing accelerated financial growth, may be adapted for television newsrooms that crave similar results.

I know of no newsroom structuring a pay platform like the one I outline.

I'm certain you'll identify reasons my platform won't work.

I'm also sure you'd be criticized initially if you were to implement my platform.

Doing so would be difficult, messy, and controversial. It would require you to have the courage to be wrong. To experiment with metrics that may or may not ultimately value performance fairly. It would require the rebalancing of metrics that were weighted in less objective manners initially. It would demand constant tinkering and yield the prospect of never being perfect.

However, it would also make your newsroom the premier destination for journalists around the world. You would completely disrupt your industry by offering the financial incentives I describe. And those incentives would be based on clear data generated by content demand on the exchange.

Hungry journalists of the highest quality would soon begin asking you for work. They would compete against one another for the opportunity to do superior work at your organization. If successful, they would make themselves wealthy only after they earn lucrative sums of advertising and sponsorship revenue for your organization.

This platform de-risks the conventional hiring model while exponentially increasing the financial rewards for each of the parties involved.

The majority lack the courage to upend their newsrooms in this manner though.

The majority will continue overpaying their poorest performing reporters while simultaneously underpaying their higher performing reporters.

The current model is not sustainable.

Not only in regard to reporter pay but also with respect to advertising, marketing, and audience creation.

Recognize it or not, the industry is in the fight of its life.

Why wouldn't you want the top fighters on your side?

And why wouldn't you create a next generation platform that provides an advantage to your fighters and your organization?

One where winning creates value for viewers, advertisers, and you.

A structure in which everyone involved can profit.

The broadcast afterlife is upon us.

The choices we make today will determine where we spend eternity.

The grave or the cloud...

Which will it be?

Resurrecting TV News

Dear Ex-Viewer,

I love you, too.
And I'm sorry I let you go.
I loved what we had.
You're right though...
I took more than I gave.
As for your new lover...
I can't blame you for choosing him.
At first I ignored him.
Then I spoke critically of him.
Afterward, I tried to be a little more like him.
But it didn't work.
I wasn't really committed.
Look, I know I was bossy.
I realize now demanding we spend time together at 5 and 6 wasn't always convenient for you.
I admit I tried to fool you into thinking the 5 and 6 were different...
But you caught me.
Still, I tried to lure, tease, and scare you into spending time with me.
All of us did. Some of us still do.
I'm sorry.
But dressing up and giving you my best four times a year is just so much easier and cheaper than doing it every day.
You're quite demanding...
But now that you're gone I realize you're worth the effort.
That's why I'm willing to change.
I don't mean a minor tweak, insignificant alteration, or marginal improvement.
I'm talking a new me.

Nick Winkler

Really.
Remember how your parents loved me?
Well I'm willing to do whatever it takes to get you to love me like they did.
I realize it won't be easy.
And it won't happen overnight.
But just wait...
Once you see the new me you'll realize everything I do is for you.
No longer will I be jealous when you hang out with others...
I realize you're a polygamist.
And that's okay with me.
I understand I have to share you now and then.
And never again will I force you to hang out when I say it's time.
You're the boss and I acknowledge that.
And I promise to stop teasing, scaring, and trying to trick you.
I'll respect you, your time, and your preferences.
Listen, I realize now I was wrong.
But if you could find it in your heart to give me a second chance I promise not to blow it again.
We can start slow.
Please?
Losing you has hurt me worse than you know.
I really do want you back.
Sometimes I feel like I might die without you.
Actually, I might.
Yes, these tears are the real thing.
I miss you.
And I love you more than ever.
Really.
It's not too late...
Is it?
-TV News

169

About the Author

Nick Winkler's work as a general assignment and investigative television news reporter has been featured on ABC, CNN, FOX News and network affiliates nationwide.

Nick's work routinely uncovered and exposed corruption, waste, and inefficiency. His investigative work has prompted legislative hearings, changes to state laws, and sent people to prison for years.

Nick's investigative work has been recognized around the country and has earned a number of awards.

Nick dearly misses David Bloom, remembers exactly where he was when Tim Russert signed off for good, and wishes Tom Brokaw would run for President.

Nick hopes one day to repay Frank Currier, a former CBS News correspondent turned journalism professor, for the years he spent coaching, mentoring, and being a friend.

Nick is also flattered reporters like Bob Faw, Robert Hager, and Boyd Huppert took the time to tear him down and rebuild him in their likenesses.

After 15 years in television news Nick started *The Winkler Group*, a strategic communications firm dedicated to helping individuals and organizations leverage the art and science of compelling storytelling to achieve their objectives.

Nick Winkler

Nick's first book, *Break Out of PR Prison: Make & Measure Your Own News in an Era of Crisis*, helps entrepreneurs, risk takers, and small businesses disrupt the storytelling process, vaccinate their reputations against crises, and measurably reduce their cost per message.

Nick's most recent book, *Resurrecting TV News: A Digital Plan for the Broadcast Afterlife*, is an attempt to help save what he fell in love with so long ago.